Introduced Trees

OF

CENTRAL CALIFORNIA

BY

WOODBRIDGE METCALF

ILLUSTRATED BY MARY B. AND FRED POMEROY
AND MARY FOLEY BENSON

UNIVERSITY OF CALIFORNIA PRESS

CONTENTS

ILLUSTRATION ON COVER: Spaeth Sycamore Maple

INTRODUCTION

This handbook is designed to assist in identifying many trees which have been brought from foreign lands and from other parts of the United States and planted in coastal, valley, and foothill areas in central California. Such planting, started in pioneer days, has continued with increasing volume as transportation facilities improved, and as new and promising species were discovered by botanical explorers. Many of the early introductions are a hundred or more years old and have grown to be stately and beautiful specimens. Some species have found the soil and climate so favorable that they have grown as well as, or occasionally better than, in their native habitats, and now rival the native trees as objects of interest and beauty. Indeed, many street and highway trees of large size have had to be removed in recent years in the interest of safety, because of overhead wires and the widening of roads to create the modern expressway system.

The modern trend in tree planting is to use ornamental species of moderate size except in parks and in spacious grounds where size is not a problem. Experiments are in progress to develop clones and hybrids which will be of the desired conformation, uniform in growth habits, and with attractive foliage and floral display. These "improved" trees are of such recent development that they are usually small or of moderate size, but older specimens may be observed in some parks and arboretum collections.

TREE COLLECTIONS

In the San Francisco Bay area there are fine collections of exotic trees in Golden Gate Park in San Francisco, especially in Strybing Arboretum; the campus of Stanford University; the grounds of Villa Montalvo in Santa Clara County; the Berkeley campus of the University of California; Knowland State Park and several city parks in Oakland; the Tilden Park Botanic Garden in the Berkeley Hills (for species introduced from mountain areas in California); and in parks and along streets in Berkeley, San Rafael, Santa Rosa, Napa, Palo Alto, San Jose, and other cities and towns in this region. The Max Watson Arboretum in San Jose includes more than one hundred species of ornamental eucalypts; small specimens of some promising clones and hybrids may be seen at Saratoga Horticultural Foundation and in many local ornamental nurseries.

In the Sacramento Valley one will be rewarded by visits to the Capitol grounds in Sacramento (eastern hardwood species are notable in the Civil War Battlefield Grove); the Davis campus of the University of California; the Bidwell Park in Chico (especially the old Chico Forestry Station plantings of 1890 to 1910), and the grounds of the U.S.D.A. Plant Introduction Gardens nearby; and many fine street trees in Chico, Marysville, Woodland, Sacramento and other Sacramento Valley towns.

In the San Joaquin Valley a notably fine tree collection is a feature of Roeding City Park in Fresno, and many exotic trees line the streets in that city and in Merced, Modesto, and Stockton. On the west side of the valley the trees in Dos Palos, Los Banos, and Patterson show good growth of a number of species under difficult conditions. Of interest also are ornamental plantings along state highways 99, 33, 40, and 50 through the Great Valley. The Institute of Forest Genetics near Placerville has the finest collection of pine species in the west, and foothill towns such as Grass Valley, Auburn, Jackson, Columbia and Mariposa show good development of some introduced trees.

Although the total number of introduced trees growing in this region probably exceeds 300, only about 200 can be considered in this handbook. This number should, however, enable the reader to identify those most commonly encountered. The trees are grouped under the general headings Coniferous Trees, Palms and their Allies, Broadleaf Evergreen Trees, and Broadleaf Deciduous Trees. Within each group the important species are described in brief terms after a discussion of the characteristics of the genus.

CONIFEROUS TREES

Known also as softwoods or resinous trees, conifers are characterized by the resinous, dark-green foliage, usually inconspicuous conelets, generally with male and female conelets on the same tree—pollination being accomplished by wind-borne pollen grains—more or less woody cones containing winged seeds, usually with a conical habit of growth, and with wood of very simple elements. In the forest they generally occur in dense stands, with excellent form and imposing height; and include species which through the ages have been of the greatest utility to man. Their resinous wood is easily manufactured into many useful products from heavy construction lumber to the finest of white pulp and paper. Many reproduce themselves easily from seed and grow rapidly to usable size when protected from fire and other enemies. A number of species are used as Christmas trees and many are fine ornamentals which thrive under California conditions.

PINE FAMILY (Pinaceae)

The Pine Family includes many of the outstanding timber trees of the northern hemisphere. Those of

[7]

importance here are treated under the genera *Abies*, the "true" firs; *Cedrus*, the "true" cedars; *Pinus*, the pines; and *Picea*, the spruces.

THE "TRUE" FIRS (*Abies*)

This genus includes about forty species throughout the northern hemisphere. Most are tall, conical, symmetrical trees with soft two-ranked sprays of needles arranged on branches which are in regular vertical whorls. The stout barrel-shaped cones are borne erect on the upper branches; they ripen the first autumn and fall apart to release two winged seeds from each cone scale. Young fir trees have for many years been favored as Christmas trees in Europe and America, and large numbers are being grown for this purpose in commercial plantations in spite of slow initial growth.

Santa Lucia Fir *(Abies bracteata, A. venusta)*

This beautiful tree has a very restricted distribution along the ridge of the Santa Lucia Mountains in California (Monterey County) from which area it has been introduced. In cultivation it becomes a tall, symmetrical, handsome specimen.

Leaves and fruit: Its stiff sharp-pointed needles, to 2½ inches long, are broader and heavier than those of any other fir. When these unfold in spring, they are bright yellow-green, in contrast with the deeper color of older foliage, marked by white lines of pores on their under sides. The erect cylindrical cones, 4 inches long, have been likened to Medusa heads from the slender, curved protruding bracts. A fine row of these trees lines the golf course road in Tilden Park in the Berkeley Hills parallel with the electric power line.

White or Concolor Fir *(Abies concolor)*

This large timber tree from the Sierra, Siskiyou and Rocky Mountains is the "true" fir most commonly seen

[8]

in cultivation here, especially in Christmas tree plantations.

Leaves and fruit: The soft, blunt gray-green needles, 1 to 1¼ inches long, are borne in flat two-ranked sprays on lower branches, but curve upward on upper branches. They are attached to the smooth gray twigs by expanded discs which leave a circular leaf scar when the leaf falls. The erect cylindrical cones, 4 to 5 inches long, change from yellow-green to purplish as they mature the first autumn and fall apart to release the seeds. The smooth gray bark on young stems is marked with blisters containing fragrant water-white "balsam," but on old trees the bark is thick, deeply furrowed, and shows brown corky layers on cut surfaces. The form of white fir from the Rocky Mountains has longer needles of a striking blue-gray color, and it grows somewhat faster when planted here.

Nordmann Fir *(Abies nordmanniana)*

This tree from Asia Minor and southern Europe has dense dark-green foliage and grows well in ornamental plantings along the coast and in the interior valleys.

Leaves and fruit: The shiny dark-green, flattened leaves are notched at the apex, about 1½ inches long, lined with silvery pores beneath, and are usually densely crowded on the twigs in four slightly upturned ranks. The erect cylindrical cones, 5 to 6 inches long, change from green to reddish brown before falling apart when mature.

Spanish Fir *(Abies pinsapo)*

This tree from the Mediterranean region is smaller and more stiffly formal in habit of growth than either of the preceding, and seems an anomaly among firs, for the foliage closely resembles that of spruce. It stands considerable heat and drought and makes an attractive ornamental.

Leaves and fruit: The sharp-pointed, dark-green,

plump needles are in radial arrangement around the twigs instead of being flattened or in slightly upturned sprays. Also, the lines of pores are less conspicuous than in most firs. The erect, purplish-brown cones become 5 inches long and half as wide before they shatter to release the winged seeds. The bark on young stems shows balsam blisters, as in the other firs.

Other true firs occasionally seen in cultivation include European Silver Fir (*A. alba, A. pectinata*), the Greek Fir (*A. cephalonica*) from the Mediterranean, the Japanese Momi Fir (*A. firma*) and the beautiful Balsam Fir (*A. balsamea*) from northeastern North America. An arboretum of true firs is being developed in Condon City Park at Grass Valley, Nevada County, where initial plantings of fourteen species were made in March, 1962. Others are being added when seedlings are available.

THE "TRUE" CEDARS (*Cedrus*)

The "true" cedars include three tall, spreading timber trees native in North Africa, Lebanon, Turkey and vicinity, and India. They all do well in California and many have developed into old and stately specimens. The erect, barrel-shaped cones closely resemble those of the "true" firs, but are more widely distributed throughout the crown instead of being clustered on the uppermost branches. The three species closely resemble one another in growth habit with intermediate forms and perhaps some hybrids. The cones ripen and fall apart the second autumn.

Atlas Cedar (*Cedrus atlantica*)

This tree from the Atlas Mountains in North Africa is generally identified by its gray-green or bluish-green foliage, erect habit of growth and small cones. Its tip is usually erect, the branches ascending, and the crown rather open.

Leaves and fruit: The slender gray-green needles are an inch or less in length, scattered singly along terminal twigs, but borne mainly in rosette-like clusters on stubby dwarf branches. The small barrel-shaped cones are borne erect on short stalks. They are 2 to 3 inches long, with flattened or recessed tips, light green in color, becoming brown and shattering the second autumn to release two winged seeds per scale.

Deodar Cedar *(Cedrus deodara)*

This large and stately timber tree of the Himalaya Mountains in India is by far the most commonly planted of the three "true" cedars throughout California. Its crown is denser than that of the preceding species, the tip is usually nodding, and many of the branches assume a drooping habit. In some specimens the weeping habit is so marked that they are called "Fountain" deodars. It is a favorite outdoor Christmas tree with notable street plantings, such as along North Van Ness Avenue in Fresno, and fine old trees are in the Capitol Grounds in Sacramento.

Leaves and fruit: The slender dark green needles, borne singly on terminal twigs or clustered on dwarf branches in the main crown, are 1 to 2 inches long and soft to the touch. The stalked, erect barrel-shaped green cones 3 to 5 inches long and half as broad, are rounded instead of concave at the tip. They appear like plump candles throughout the crown; they mature the second autumn when they fall apart to release plump, winged seeds.

Cedar of Lebanon *(Cedrus libanensis* or *C. libani)*

This is the tree mentioned in the Bible that supplied the timbers for the temple in Jerusalem, and its silhouette is used on the flag of Lebanon where it is native as well as in the mountains of Turkey. It is less commonly planted in California than either of the other "true" cedars, and is intermediate in many of its characteristics. In general appearance it more closely resembles the Atlas cedar in being erect and open-crowned, usually with ascending branches and erect tip.

Leaves and fruit: The slender dark green needles are about 1 inch in length and the stalked, barrel-shaped cones, 3½ to 4 inches long and flattened at the tip are intermediate between the other two. However, some trees are difficult to identify.

These three cedars are fine ornamental trees which have demonstrated hardiness and freedom from cultural problems throughout this region. However they grow to large size and are not suitable for restricted areas or small yards.

THE PINES (*Pinus*)

The pines include more than eighty species widely distributed throughout the northern hemisphere, often in timber stands of vast extent and value. Hence this is the most important genus of conifers. Pines may be recognized by their long slender needles, usually in bundles of two to five, surrounded at the base by a sheath of papery scales; and by their woody, and often heavy cones that require two or more growing seasons to mature the seeds, which are borne two to the cone scale. The largest collection of planted pines in America is at the Institute of Forest Genetics of the United States Forest Service, near Placerville, California.

Twelve species of introduced pines are considered here; the following tabulation will aid in their identification. However, a number of other pine species may be met with in the field, including several native pines which are extensively planted in this region.

Lodgepole Pine (*Pinus contorta*)
This pine is native along the northern Pacific Coast

from Mendocino County to Alaska (where it is known as Shore Pine), in Washington and British Columbia, and extensively throughout high mountain country in the Cascades, Rockies, and the Sierra (where it is sometimes known as Tamarac Pine). The coastal variety is a small slender tree which grows on sand dunes and slopes exposed to severe ocean winds. The mountain form is taller and occurs in dense stands after fires.

Leaves and fruit: The twisted dark green needles, 2 inches long, form a dense dark symmetrical crown which makes an excellent Christmas tree. The stalked, prickly cones, borne in whorls around the stem, are 2 inches long and asymmetrical. Many remain closed for a year or more after ripening, thus providing stored seed for reforestation after fires.

Dwarf or Mugo Pine *(Pinus mugo)*

This tiny and often shrub-like ornamental tree is a dwarf form of the Swiss Mountain Pine, *P. montana,* of Europe. It is rarely more than five feet tall with a nicely rounded crown of dense foliage, and is commonly used in garden and shrubbery planting.

Leaves and fruit: The slender, dark green needles, up to 2 inches long, are densely crowded on slender branchlets. The tiny, symmetrical cones, up to 2 inches long, are ovoid in shape, light brown in color, and without prickles on the scales. There are several varietal forms of the tree, which in its native habitat may reach a height of 75 feet or more.

Scot's Pine *(Pinus sylvestris)*

This pine has an extensive range throughout Europe where it is an important timber species. It has a rather open crown and often a spreading habit of growth. It may usually be identified by the orange-yellow color of the upper bark. It grows rapidly when young

Characteristics of Introduced Pine Species

Species	Needles	Cones	Remarks
		Needles in bundles of 2	
Lodgepole Pine *P. contorta*	to 2 inches, dark green	2 inches, prickly, persistent	small, slender, dense tree, California high mountains
Dwarf Pine *P. mugo*	to 2 inches, slender	2 inches, globular, without prickles	dwarf, often a round-headed shrub, dense foliage
Scot's Pine *P. sylvestris*	to 3 inches, stiff, twisted	2½ inches, square scales, not prickly	yellow upper bark, gray-green folliage
Japanese Black Pine *P. thunbergii*	to 4½ inches, stout, twisted	3 inches, symmetrical, not prickly	foliage light yellow-green, silky white buds
Japanese Red Pine *P. densiflora*	5 inches, slender, bluish, not dense	2 inches, stalked, not prickly, persistent	irregular form, one type spreading, umbrella-like
Austrian Pine *P. nigra*	to 6½ inches, stiff, dense and bushy	3½ inches, ovoid, not prickly, symmetrical	erect, good form, tan colored buds
Italian Stone Pine *P. pinea*	to 7 inches, slender	to 5 inches, globular, not prickly	reddish-brown bark, broad umbrella-like crown
Maritime Pine *P. pinaster*	to 9 inches, stiff, glossy, dark green	to 7 inches, conic-ovoid, not prickly	dark red-brown bark

	Needles mostly in bundles of 2, occasionally 3		
Aleppo Pine *P. halepensis*	to 4 inches, slender, light green	to 3 inches, stalked, not prickly, persistent	light gray branches, spreading crown
var. *brutia*	longer, stiffer	4 inches, stalked, persistent	erect conical form
	Needles in bundles of 3		
Canary Island Pine *P. canariensis*	to 10 inches, pendent, dark green	to 8 inches, heavy	tall, erect tree with good form
Mexican Weeping Pine *P. patula*	8 to 10 inches, slender light green, weeping	4½ inches, conic	thin, wispy foliage
	Needles in bundles of 5		
Bhutan Pine *P. wallichiana*	to 8 inches, slender, blue-green	to 10 inches, slender, pendant, unarmed	soft foliage, attractive crown
Torrey Pine *P. torreyana*	to 13 inches, stiff, gray-green	to 6 inches, globular, not prickly	coastal only, not frost hardy

Eastern White Pine, *P. strobus*, with slender, blue-green, soft needles in fives is occasionally seen in cultivation. It has stalked, pendent, finger-like, unarmed cones.

under a wide variety of conditions, and has achieved wide popularity as a plantation Christmas tree throughout the United States and Canada.

Leaves and fruit: The needles, borne two to a bundle, are up to 3 inches long and usually show a decided twist. They are variable in color from bluish- to yellowish-green and some races show marked yellowing of foliage with the approach of cold weather, but these resume their normal color the following spring. The 2½-inch cones are conical, the scales near the base are notably square in outline, and they are not armed with prickles. This tree begins cone production at an early age which is an added attraction in the Christmas season.

Japanese Black Pine *(Pinus thunbergii)*

This hardy and attractive tree is an important timber species in Japan, and is being extensively planted in California as an ornamental. It grows well under a variety of conditions and may be pruned to assume unusual shapes. A major point of identification is the silky-white buds.

Leaves and fruit: The stout yellow-green needles are in bundles of two, slightly twisted, and from 4 to 4½ inches long. The 3-inch, ovoid, symmetrical, unarmed cones are borne in whorls and are an attractive feature of even young trees. Since they persist for some time after ripening and shedding the seeds, cones may easily be observed at all stages from flower to open cone.

Japanese Red Pine *(Pinus densiflora)*

This is another timber tree of Japan with a more open crown which is often trained into contorted shapes; one variety with multiple branches assumes the shape of an umbrella. In this region it does not grow as vigorously or make as attractive a specimen as the preceding species, but it is planted for its grotesque form and masses of persistent cones.

Leaves and fruit: The slender, 5-inch, bluish-green needles are borne two to a bundle on sparsely foliaged twigs. The stalked, globular, unarmed cones, about 2 inches long, persist for several years after the seed is shed.

Austrian or European Black Pine *(Pinus nigra)*

This is an important timber species with a wide distribution in central Europe. It has a dense, bushy crown, a good habit of growth, and is hardy throughout this region, but has not been extensively planted. It is coming into popularity as a Christmas tree. Large tan-colored buds are quite conspicuous.

Leaves and fruit: The stout, stiff yellow-green needles are 6½ inches long, two to a bundle, and tufted at the ends of branches. The ovoid, symmetrical, unarmed cones, 3 to 3½ inches long, are borne laterally on the twigs.

Italian Stone Pine *(Pinus pinea)*

This tree with a broad umbrella-shaped crown, often seen in pictures of Italy and the Mediterranean, makes rapid and satisfactory growth throughout this region and is a feature of many parks and gardens where there is sufficient room for its spreading crown when mature. Large and beautiful specimens can be seen west of the State Capitol in Sacramento.

Leaves and fruit: The slender needles, borne two to a cluster, are 5 to 7 inches long and form a very dense deep green crown. They are shed in great quantity along with the male conelets, making deep litter under the trees through much of the year. The globular, unarmed cones turn from green, through shades of purple, to rich shiny brown when ripe. They are about 5 inches in diameter and about the size and shape of a baseball. The large seeds are rich in oil, which in Italy is extracted for use in salad dressing.

Maritime or Cluster Pine *(Pinus pinaster)*

The Maritime Pine is a tall, rapid-growing tree of Europe with deep red-brown bark which achieved fame in the control of shifting sand dunes in the Landes district in France. There and in Spain it is an important source of lumber, turpentine, rosin and tar. It is hardy and fast-growing, but is not long lived in California.

Leaves and fruit: The heavy, glossy dark green needles, up to 9 inches long, form a very dense and dark crown. The 7-inch conic-ovoid cones have blunt points on the scales. They turn brown when they mature the second autumn, falling from the tree soon after releasing the winged seeds.

Aleppo Pine *(Pinus halepensis)*

This species from the eastern Mediterranean and north Africa and the variety *P. h. brutia,* with a taller and more upright form, are remarkable for their ability to survive under hot dry conditions, and are being extensively used in California lowland areas. They have open gray-green foliage on smooth-barked gray branchlets.

Leaves and fruit: The slender, gray-green 3 inch needles are usually in twos, but many bundles of three may be found. The stalked 3-inch cones turn shiny brown when mature and persist on the tree for years after shedding the winged seeds. The variety *P. brutia* has longer leaves, larger cones, and a better form.

Canary Island Pine *(Pinus canariensis)*

This stately pine from the islands of that name, is

one of the most strikingly beautiful conifers planted in this region. It has a tall conical habit of growth, and the somewhat drooping foliage seems arranged in horizontal tiers. Although occasionally injured by

Figure 1 Canary Island Pine

frost, it has a remarkable ability to sprout a new crown unless the temperature has been too low. Thus it does best along the coast.

Leaves and fruit: The stout yellow-green leaves, borne three in a bundle, are up to 10 inches long and somewhat drooping in habit, forming a dense and attractive crown. When the orange-red male conelets appear in dense clusters below the terminal buds, they make a pretty display. The large symmetrical cones, borne laterally on the twigs, change from green to brown as they ripen the second autumn. The cone scales are tipped with blunt bosses.

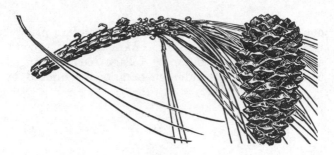

Figure 2 Canary Island Pine, needles and cone

Weeping Mexican Pine or **Jelicote Pine** *(Pinus patula)*
A fairly recent introduction from Mexico, this tree has an unusual appearance with an open crown of delicate, light green pendent foliage. Most specimens are small and irregular in growth habit.

Leaves and fruit: The slender light green needles, up to 10 inches long, hang in pendent clusters from the spreading branches, giving the tree a lacy appearance. The ovoid cones are 4½ inches long.

Bhutan or **Himalayan Pine** *(Pinus wallichiana)*
This mountain white pine from northern India has been known by the synonyms *P. excelsa, P. nepalensis* and *P. griffithii*. In the Himalayas it becomes a large timber tree with easily worked soft wood. In California it is usually seen as a graceful erect tree from 30 to 60 feet tall, with spreading branches and pendent cones.

Leaves and fruit: The slender blue-green or gray-green leaves, borne in drooping clusters of five, are marked with white lines of pores. Usually 6 to 10 inches long and soft to the touch, the leaves make attractive sprays of foliage. The slender, stalked cones, 8 to 10 inches long, are borne singly or in groups of two or three toward the ends of the horizontal branches. They are pendent, long-stalked with unarmed cone scales and are about the size and shape of our native Western White Pine cones.

Eastern White Pine *(Pinus strobus)*

This fine timber species from northeastern America is occasionally planted here, but usually requires summer irrigation to persist for many years. In the virgin forests of the Lake States and adjacent Canada it produced some of the softest and finest lumber ever cut by man.

Leaves and fruit: Its slender blue-green, 3- to 5-inch needles are in bundles of five, and the sprays of foliage are soft to the touch and ornamental. The stalked, slender, "finger-type" unarmed cones, up to 4 inches in length, are borne in pendent position toward the ends of the horizontal branches. When well grown it makes an attractive garden specimen and is a symmetrical and popular Christmas tree.

THE SPRUCES (Genus Picea)

The spruces have the same upright conical habit of growth as the firs, from which they are distinguished by the plump, four-angled, usually stiff and sharp-pointed needles which stand out all around the twigs, forming a cylindrical instead of a flattened spray of foliage. Young bark does not contain balsam blisters, and bark of old trees flakes off in saucer-like plates. The cones are pendent and do not fall apart to release the seeds, but the scales open when mature, the first autumn, to release two winged seeds from beneath each cone scale. Each needle is set on a persistent leaf base (peg) which remains on the twig when the needle falls; thus the twigs are very rough in contrast to the smooth twigs of the firs.

Thirty or more spruces are widely distributed throughout much of the northern hemisphere, and some species have been separated into a number of landscape varieties. Three spruces are native in California, but none occur naturally in this region. Spruce lumber is even-grained, light in weight, and very strong. The wood is of major importance also in the manufacture of pulp and paper. The following five species are most commonly planted in this region.

Colorado Blue Spruce *(Picea pungens)*
This is a favorite hardy ornamental with fine conical form and dense, compact crown, and is from the

Figure 3 Colorado Blue Spruce

southern Rocky Mountains. It is slow-growing, but stands considerable drought, heat, and wind, as well as cold weather, so it is widely cultivated throughout much of the northern and central United States.

Leaves and fruit: The stout four-angled needles, spreading in all directions, are an inch or more in length and very sharp-pointed. They are gray-green to silvery blue, and occur on rough, tan-colored twigs which are not hairy between the pegs. The pendent cones, 2½ to 4 inches long, are made up of spirally arranged, thin, crepe-paperlike cone scales which change from green to tan when they ripen the first autumn to release the small winged seeds.

Norway Spruce *(Picea abies* or *P. excelsa)*

This spruce, from Europe, is said to be the most widely planted conifer throughout the United States. It has a formal conical crown of ascending branches and gracefully drooping branchlets. It succeeds best along the northern coast, but will grow in interior valleys with irrigation. It is one of the traditional Christmas trees of Europe. A number of horticultural varieties are recognized.

Leaves and fruit: The four-angled dark green leaves are usually ¾ inch or less in length, and the tips are less sharp than in the preceding species. Pendent cones, up to 7 inches long, with stiff cone scales, are borne at the ends of branchlets in the upper crown and ripen the first autumn.

Himalayan or Weeping Spruce *(Picea smithiana)*

This is a tall timber tree, up to 150 feet in height in its native India. Here it is usually smaller and is distinguished by its spreading crown and gracefully weeping twigs; the effect is less dense than in most other spruces. It grows well away from the coast with summer irrigation.

[23]

Leaves and fruit: The slender four-angled needles are gray-green 1½ to 2 inches long, borne on smooth-barked pendent branchlets. Lines of pores appear on all four of the needle faces. The handsome pendent cones are 5 to 7 inches long, with stiff, entire scales.

Sitka or **Tideland Spruce** *(Picea sitchensis)*
This is a massive timber tree native from Mendocino County, California, to Alaska, reaching 200 feet or more in height. It is very important for lumber and pulp. The tree grows rapidly with some irrigation and develops an open conical crown of ascending branches and somewhat pendent branchlets. It needs protection from spruce aphis. It succeeds fairly well in coastal areas here, but not in valleys.
Leaves and fruit: The slender, spiny-pointed gray-green needles are somewhat flattened and show silvery lines of pores above. The pendent 4-inch cones are made up of crinkled, papery scales which resemble those of the Colorado Blue Spruce.

Oriental Spruce *(Picea orientalis)*
This spruce, from Asia Minor and the Caucasus, is a favorite ornamental tree in parks and gardens because of its dense conical crown, attractive cones, and hardiness under local conditions.
Leaves and fruit: The dark green needles are blunt-pointed, four-angled, and the shortest of all locally grown spruces, ¼ to ½ inch long. The needles, usually curved against the twigs, have fine lines of pores on all four faces. The twigs are usually quite hairy. The small 2- to 3-inch cones have scales with entire margins.

REDWOOD FAMILY (Taxodiaceae)
The Redwood Family includes some of the largest,

oldest, and most stately trees of the world, divided into eight or more genera found in China, Tasmania, Japan, and North America. The linear leaves are in spiral arrangement, usually somewhat flattened, and fall from the tree attached to the ultimate twigs. The small globular woody cones usually have several seeds beneath each cone scale. Two genera are deciduous.

Sugi or **Cryptomeria** (*Cryptomeria japonica*)

This is a stately and important timber tree from Japan which closely resembles our Coast Redwood in foliage, bark, and wood, as well as in crown form and habit of growth. It grows well here to a height of 30 to 50 feet, with erect form and conical crown.

Figure 4 Sugi

Leaves and fruit: The awl-like, dark blue-green leaves, ¾ to 1 inch long, are keeled on both sides. They are spirally arranged on the twigs and resemble those of the Sierra Redwood. The globular 1-inch cones are similar to those of the Coast Redwood, but each cone scale bears a small leafy appendage. They appear at the twig ends and ripen the first autumn.

The cultivated variety *"Elegans,"* the Plume Sawara, has softer and more feathery light green foliage which assumes deep copper-red tones in winter. It is more widely planted than the species, and becomes

[25]

a plumelike, soft-foliaged pyramid up to about 20 feet in height. It does not bear cones.

China Fir *(Cunninghamia lanceolata)*

This is a Chinese species of moderate size with spiny-tipped foliage which resembles that of Bunya Bunya Araucaria, but the branches droop at the ends and the cones are small and pendent.

Leaves and fruit: The flattened, stiff, sharp-pointed leaves, 1½ to 2 inches long, are bright green above and marked with broad bands of white pores beneath. They have finely toothed margins and are arranged in flat sprays. The stalked, globular 2-inch cones have thick, pointed scales and are borne in drooping clusters near the branch ends. Flowers are in catkins of two kinds.

Umbrella Pine *(Sciadopitys verticillata)*

This tree from central Japan may reach 40 or more feet in height in its native country, but is usually a smaller specimen here. It grows slowly, but the unusual foliage makes it an attractive garden specimen.

Leaves and fruit: Leaves are of two kinds: small scalelike leaves, scattered along the twigs and denser near the tips, and linear leaves, 3 to 6 inches long, borne at the twig ends in parasol-like whorls of ten to twenty-five. They are furrowed at the sides, shiny dark green above, notched at the tip, and marked below by a white band of pores. The ovoid-shaped cones are 3 to 5 inches long, with woody scales. They mature the second autumn.

Sierra Redwood *(Sequoia gigantea* or *Sequoiadendron giganteum)*

This tree from the California mountains was not found naturally along the coast or at elevations below 4,000 feet. However, it grows easily and rapidly from seed (never from sprouts, as does the Coast Redwood) and has been widely planted throughout the region for many years. As a young tree it forms a symmetrical cone of great beauty, and is now being grown in

Figure 5 Sierra Redwood

plantations as a Christmas tree. As an older tree its erect habit of growth, fibrous light brown trunk bark, and feathery conical crown make it a notable specimen.

Leaves and fruit: The awl-like bright gray-green leaves are spirally arranged on the twigs to form dense, rounded masses of foliage. They are ½ inch long, tapering to sharp points. The bright green oval cones, 2½ to 4 inches long, require two years to mature; many of them remain unopened for several years until cut by squirrels or brought down from the old trees by storms. Each cone contains about a hundred symmetrically winged seeds, light tan in color, which occur in clusters beneath the heavy shield-shaped cone scales.

Bald Cypress (*Taxodium distichum*)

This is a deciduous timber tree from the swamps and moist lowlands of the lower Mississippi Valley and adjacent eastern coast. It has an attractive pyramidal crown of lacy foliage, and an erect trunk

[27]

clothed with fibrous light brown bark. It grows well here with irrigation, and in moist situations some trees form the "knees" typical of the southern swamp country.

Leaves and fruit: The narrowly linear leaves, ½ to ¾ inch long, are light green in spring, arranged in soft flat sprays on which they remain after they turn yellow-brown and are shed in autumn. The globular green cones, 1 inch in diameter, consist of shield-shaped woody cones which turn brown and fall apart easily to release a few large irregular-shaped seeds. The twigs and branchlets are alternate in arrangement.

Dawn Redwood *(Metasequoia glyptostroboides)*

This is the most recently discovered member of its ancient family. It was located and described in central China about 1946. Since then it has been sparingly planted as an interesting deciduous conifer along the Pacific Coast. It is much more like the Bald Cypress than the Redwood in the appearance of its lacy foliage and deciduous habit, but the twigs are opposite in arrangement in this species. It is easily propagated from twig cuttings placed in coarse, moist soil, as well as from seeds, and has demonstrated its adaptability to conditions in this region. Some trees in this area have grown to heights of 30 to 35 feet in about twenty years.

Leaves and fruit: The soft, flat light green needles, ½ to ¾ inch long, appear in spring. These sprays of foliage turn yellow-brown and are shed in autumn. The tiny ½-inch globular cones are made up of spirally arranged, entire, papery scales which turn light tan the first autumn and release very small winged seeds.

CYPRESS AND JUNIPER FAMILY (Cupressaceae)
The members of this family usually have opposite

or whorled, scalelike or awl-like leaves, often completely concealing the twigs, which have a ropelike
appearance. The small cones, usually 1 inch or less
in length, have opposite or whorled, fibrous or woody
scales with winged seeds; or are succulent and berry-
like with hard, wingless seeds. Nine genera are widely
distributed in both northern and southern hemispheres, including important timber trees and many
fine ornamentals with dozens of horticultural forms
some with variegated or golden foliage.

Port Orford Cedar or Lawson Cypress (*Chamaecyparis lawsoniana*)

This is a large and important timber tree of Oregon
and the northern California coast, valued for its fine-
grained, aromatic, and durable white wood. It is in

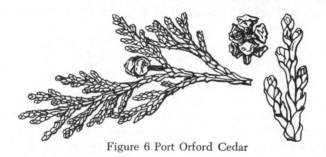

Figure 6 Port Orford Cedar

wide use as an ornamental for its conical form, pendent leaves, and dense foliage on gracefully drooping
branches. There are many horticultural varieties, and
it has been a favorite ornamental tree in this region
for many years.

Leaves and fruit: The tiny scalelike blue-green
leaves are opposite in pairs. Their bases clasp the
twig, and each leaf is marked by a glandlike pit. The
globular cones, ⅜ inch in diameter, borne in great
profusion, change from bluish-purple to shiny brown

when they mature the first autumn. They consist of seven shield-shaped scales enclosing many small symmetrically winged seeds.

Of the many horticultural forms, three seem to be most popular. One is a tall columnar tree with golden-tipped foliage, the Stewart Golden. A slow-growing dwarf form with graceful vertical sprays of foliage is (cult. var.) *"Allumi,"* the Scarab Cypress. Another, with soft, slender, feathery blue-green leaves and narrow columnar habit of growth is (cult. var.) *"Ellwoodii,"* the Ellwood Cypress. There are many others, some of which resemble the Japanese species.

Hinoki Cypress *(Chamaecyparis obtusa)*

This is a small tree, 10 to 30 feet tall, with horizontal branches and drooping branchlets in horizontal planes. The blunt leaves are bright green above and lined with white beneath, and glands are not conspicuous. The globose cones, ¼ to ⅜ inch in diameter, are made up of eight to ten scales, each having two (rarely up to five) seeds beneath.

Sawara Cypress *(Chamaecyparis pisifera)*

This is an even smaller garden tree from Japan, from 6 to 20 feet tall, with dark green foliage on short horizontal branches forming a narrow upright crown. The leaves differ from the preceding species in being more spreading and in having pointed tips. The tiny globular cones, ¼ inch or less in diameter, contain very small seeds.

THE CYPRESSES *(Cupressus)*

A number of native and introduced species of cypress were formerly in wide use as ornamental trees and hedges throughout California, but all are more or less subject to the cypress canker, *Coryneum cardinale,* and a bark beetle, particularly in areas near the coast, and many died. The cypresses include fourteen species distributed from the southwest to Mexico and from the Mediterranean to southeast Asia. They have dense foliage consisting of ropelike twigs with scalelike leaves opposite in pairs; the leaves are usually marked by glandular pits. The globular cones are larger than those of *Chamaecyparis,* with several pairs of shield-shaped woody cone scales enclosing several irregularly shaped brown or black seeds beneath. They mature the second autumn. Most species stand pruning well.

Besides the two species considered below, occasional trees of the following may be encountered: *Cupressus guadalupensis* (*C. forbesii*), from Orange County to Mexico; *C. lusitanica,* from Mexico; *C. torulosa,* from the Himalayas; and *C. funebris,* from China, which bears a thin crown of slender weeping branches.

Arizona Cypress (*Cupressus glabra* or *C. arizonica*)

This is a dry-country tree found in scattered locations from west Texas through Arizona to southern California. It has a dense, upright conical crown and smooth red-brown bark on trunk and limbs; or sometimes fibrous brown bark on the trunk. Because of its outstanding ability to withstand drought, heat, and poor soil, it is popular in dry areas for use in windbreaks, hedges, and landscape planting. It stands pruning, and is being grown in some quantity as a Christmas tree.

Leaves and fruit: The scalelike leaves are gray-green, bluish-green, or silvery, arranged opposite in pairs and tightly clasping the cordlike twigs. The back of each leaf is marked by a white dorsal pit. The globular cones, made up of six to eight shield-shaped woody scales, are ⅞ to 1¼ inches in diameter. They change from green to gray to brown during the year, and release irregularly shaped, winged seeds when they mature in autumn.

Italian Cypress *(Cupressus sempervirens)*

This slender columnar tree, which is so prominent a feature of the landscape in Mediterranean countries, is probably the most widely planted of all cypresses in this region. Hardy and fast-growing, it reaches a

Figure 7 Italian Cypress

height of 30 to 50 feet and is used wherever a narrow, erect accent tree is needed; it is especially common in cemetery plantings. It usually has almost vertical branches; (cult. var.) *"Horizontalis,"* has short branches, but the crown is still erect and slender. In both foliage and cones the Italian Cypress is similar to the native Monterey Cypress, but its vertical crown form is distinctive.

Leaves and fruit: The scalelike dark green leaves are opposite in pairs and are closely appressed to the cordlike twigs. The woody globular cones, 1 to 1½ inches in diameter, made up of six to eight shield-shaped scales, ripen to release many small brownish seeds.

THE ARBORVITAES (*Thuja*)

Three species of arborvitae (also called cedar) are commonly planted throughout this region: one from northeastern America, one from the north Pacific Coast, and one from China. Each has a number of horticultural forms, but all have flat sprays of foliage, usually yellow-green, consisting of oppositely arranged, overlapping scalelike leaves having a pleasing aromatic fragrance, and small cones with six to twelve leathery cone scales bearing two seeds per scale. The light brown trunk bark is fibrous and thin; the brownish heartwood is aromatic and durable in the ground. Some of the many horticultural varieties are difficult to identify.

Giant Arborvitae, or Western Red Cedar (*Thuja plicata*)

This is a timber tree of massive size which is native along the Pacific Coast from northern California to British Columbia and inland to the northern Rocky Mountains. Its durable light brown wood splits and machines easily and is of wide importance for poles, piling, shakes, shingles, and lumber. Trees in cultivation here are usually of small to medium size; the horticultural varieties are globe-shaped and have denser foliage than trees of similar size in the wild.

[33]

Leaves and fruit: The plump, scalelike light green leaves, arranged in four ranks as opposite pairs, clasp and conceal the stems. The tip of each leaf is free, the bases overlap, and the back is marked by a glandular depression. The variety *aurea* has gold-tipped foliage. Small green cones, borne in clusters on the ultimate twigs, are reflexed against the drooping foliage spray in an upright position. These, scarcely ½ inch long, consist of eight to ten thin leathery scales with tiny recurved tips. The cones ripen and turn brown the first autumn to release ¼-inch papery seeds which are winged all around except for an apical notch. Spent cones remain on the twigs during much of the following summer.

American Arborvitae or Northern White Cedar *(Thuja occidentalis)*

This tree, from the northeastern United States and Canada, is smaller, but of economic importance throughout that region for posts, poles, and lumber. Its foliage sprays, flatter than those of *T. plicata*, are often in horizontal arrangement, forming a narrow, dense pyramidal crown, but this is variable in the horticultural varieties.

Leaves and fruit: The leaves, borne in opposite arrangement on the flat branchlets, are bright green above and yellowish beneath: those on terminal shoots are glandular and long-pointed; those on lateral twigs, with short points and often without glands. The ovoid tan-colored cones are borne in clusters on terminal twigs, are ½ inch or less in length, and consist of six to ten thin scales without pointed tips. The seeds have thin wings.

False Arborvitae or Japanese Cedar *(Thujopsis dolobrata)*

This is a small slow-growing tree from Japan which

is occasionally planted as an unusual specimen. The foliage resembles that of the thujas, but is much coarser. The coarse, plump leaves, borne opposite in pairs, are bright green above and white or silvery beneath. The cones, about ½ inch long, have flat woody scales and small seeds.

THE JUNIPERS (*Juniperus*)

The junipers are aromatic evergreen shrubs or trees, closely related to the cypresses and so similar to them that some forms are difficult to identify. Some thirty-five species are distributed throughout the northern hemisphere, with *Juniperus communis,* the Common Juniper, having the most extensive range, mostly as a low branching shrub. Four species are native to the Pacific Coast, but these are rarely cultivated. Leaves are of two kinds: sharp-pointed in whorls of three or two with white lines; and mature foliage, usually scalelike, clasping the cordlike twigs. Male and female flowers usually occur on different trees. The female ripens the first, second, or third year; the fleshy scales join to make a globular berry-like fruit containing one to a few plump, hard, and wingless seeds. There are many horticultural forms, some with silvery foliage; many prostrate or low-growing types are used in border plantings or as ground covers.

Chinese Juniper (*Juniperus chinensis*)

This tree, from China and Japan, is the one most commonly planted here in a number of attractive ornamental forms. It is a small tree, 10 to 30 feet tall, with a pyramidal or irregular upright habit of growth.

Leaves and fruit: Juvenile leaves are in threes, linear with tapered tips, spreading from the branches and marked with white lines above. Adult leaves are scalelike, dark green, borne opposite in pairs and closely coating the cordlike twigs. The small brown-

[35]

ish-purple berries, ¼ inch in diameter, require two seasons to mature.

The most popular form of this tree is (cult. var.) *"Torulosa,"* known as Hollywood Juniper, which grows as a wavy green column with twisted, short branches. Another widely used prostrate form is (cult. var.) *"Pfitzeriana,"* Pfitzer Juniper, said to be one of the most important ornamental evergreens ever produced, and in extensive use throughout America. An erect conical form with blue foliage (cult. var.) *"Columnaris,"* is also popular. There are many other horticultural forms of Chinese Juniper.

Eastern Red Cedar *(Juniperus virginiana)*

This is a small tree, 30 to 50 feet tall, with wide distribution in the eastern and central United States, where it is one of the first trees to occupy old fields. It has an erect conical form of feathery, light foliage with a number of natural and horticultural varieties, some with dark green foliage, others light gray to silvery in appearance. All respond well to pruning. This is a popular Christmas tree in many localities.

Leaves and fruit: The leaves are in whorls of three: the juvenile are spreading and spiny-pointed; the adult, overlapping and closely appressed to the twigs. The globular bright-blue berries, ¼ to ⅓ inch in diameter, ripen the first year (only on female trees).

One of the most hardy and popular forms is (cult. var.) *"Glauca,"* the Silver Red Cedar, which can be trimmed to form a densely foliaged silvery cone of great beauty. Another is (cult. var.) *"Elegantissima,"* The Goldtip Red Cedar, or Golden Juniper, with bronze-green leaves overlaid with pale yellow.

Canary Island Juniper *(Juniperus cedrus)*

This is a small tree, 20 feet tall, with feathery,

drooping light green foliage which does well in coastal areas but will not stand much cold.

Savin (*Juniperus sabina*)
This is a shrubby type, from southern Europe to Asia, with a number of horticultural forms, the most popular of which is the variety *tamariscifolia*, known as Juniper Tam. It is widely used in this area in border plantings and as a ground cover.

Other junipers with horticultural forms used in ornamental planting include *J. communis*, Common Juniper; *J. horizontalis*, Creeping Juniper; *J. scopulorum*, Rocky Mountain Juniper; and *J. squamata*, Meyer Juniper—each with a number of varieties.

GINKGO FAMILY (Ginkgoaceae)
This ancient family had several rather widely dis-

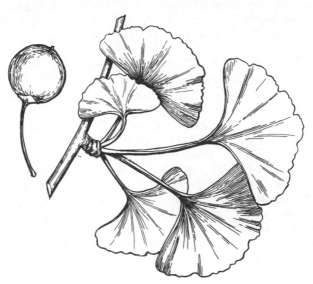

Figure 8 Maidenhair Tree

[37]

tributed species in past geologic ages, but all have disappeared but one. The fan-shaped deciduous leaves with parallel veins and stalked, olive-like fruits on pistillate trees are characteristic.

Maidenhair Tree or Ginkgo (*Ginkgo biloba*)

This is a hardy tree of slow growth and good form from China. New upright types are now being developed by vegetative propagation from male trees. One of the new improved types is called "Autumn Gold" from the bright and lasting color of the leaves.

Leaves and fruit: The light green leaves are 4 to 5 inches long, with a fan-shaped blade on a long stalk; the center of the fan is notched. Clustered on short, stubby branchlets, they are attractive throughout the growing season. The foliage turns bright yellow in autumn before the leaves fall, to make a golden carpet on the lawn. The stalked, olive-like fruits have a disagreeable odor when crushed; so most trees are now grown from male tree cuttings.

ARAUCARIA FAMILY (Araucariaceae)

Trees in this family from the southern hemisphere have a strikingly symmetrical habit of growth, resinous wood, attractive foliage, and heavy, erect cones bearing one seed per cone scale. The cones fall apart when mature to scatter the plump seeds.

Monkey Puzzle (*Araucaria araucana* or *A. imbricata*)

This Chilean species is a grotesque tree with heavy trunk and stout up-curving branches in regular whorls. Trunk and branches are so well sheathed by the heavy, sharp-pointed leaves that no animal can climb them. It is the most frost-hardy species of the araucarias, and makes an interesting ornamental specimen for special situations.

Leaves and fruit: The dark green leaves, up to 2

inches long by 1 inch wide, are thick, leathery, closely overlapping, and so stiff and sharp-pointed that they are a formidable armament. They overlap and completely surround the cylindrical branches, and persist for some years. Oval or globular cones are 5 to 8 inches long, but are rarely seen here as they are borne only on older trees of large size.

Bunya Bunya or Bunyan Pine *(Araucaria bidwilli)*

This is a timber tree of good size occurring in a limited area in southeast Queensland, Australia, at elevations from 500 to 3,500 feet, as a dominant tree over mixed hardwood species in humid rain forests. Here it develops a broadly conical or rounded crown of heavy horizontal or up-curving branches, clothed toward their ends with glossy foliage. Its sweeping branches and height of 75 feet or more make it a fine specimen tree for parks and large lawns. It does not stand severe frost.

Leaves and fruit: The flat, sharp-pointed leaves are spirally arranged on the twigs, but appear to be in two ranks because of the twisting of their short stalks. They are 1 to 2½ inches long by about ½ inch wide, shiny dark green above, lighter green and not so shiny beneath. The heavy, erect, pineapple-like cones, 8 to 10 inches long by 6 to 8 inches wide, consist of thick deciduous scales, often 3 inches wide, containing a single large seed about 2 inches long and half as wide. They were used as food by the natives in Australia.

Norfolk Island Pine *(Araucaria heterophylla* or *A. excelsa)*

The Star Pine from Norfolk Island in the Pacific is a beautifully symmetrical tree, reaching a height of 75 feet or more, with precise conical habit of growth and whorls of branches in regular starlike arrangement. It is a strikingly formal specimen for gardens and is often used as a tub tree when small. It succeeds best in areas near the coast.

Figure 9 Norfolk Island Pine

Leaves and fruit: The rich green leaves are soft to the touch and are so densely arranged on the twigs as to give them a slender cylindrical appearance. They are ½ inch long by ⅛ inch wide, triangular in cross section, with a barely distinguishable midrib, and they curve inward toward the blunt-pointed tips. Globular cones 4 to 6 inches long are occasionally seen on trees of mature age and size.

New Caledonian Pine *(Araucaria columnaris)*

This is similar to the preceding species, but has somewhat denser and more tufted foliage, especially on trees of good size. It is occasionally seen here.

YEW FAMILY (Taxaceae)

This family contains only two genera of evergreen trees, *Taxus* and *Torreya*, each with a small number of species; the first is much more commonly used in cultivation. Both genera usually have male and female flowers on different trees. Foliage in *Taxus* is deep green above and lighter beneath; the fruit is a succulent bright-red cup surrounding a single hard-shelled seed, resembling an egg in an egg cup. Leaves in *Torreya* are longer, light yellow-green in color, and sharp-pointed, and the fruit is an olive-like drupe. *Cephalotaxus*, the Plum Yew, from China and Japan, is now classified as a separate family; it is quite similar in appearance, but very rare in cultivation here.

English Yew *(Taxus baccata)*

This is the famous tree from Europe and Asia which provided the tough, elastic wood for the longbows of medieval archers. Because of its dense foliage it makes a good specimen tree or an effective hedge. Yews are easily trimmed and are favorites for topiary work. The bark is thin and red. Several horticultural forms are recognized, the most popular of which is the variety *hibernica*, with columnar habit, used in formal plantings; there are variegated and golden forms also.

Leaves and fruit: The leaves are ¾ to 1¼ inches long, spirally arranged on the twig, but bent to appear in two ranks like the Coast Redwood. They are very dark green above and lighter green beneath. The fruit, which is borne sparingly on female trees, is an attractive, succulent, bright-red berry in the shape of an open cup surrounding a single bony seed. The tree needs consistent summer irrigation.

Japanese Yew *(Taxus cuspidata)*
This species from Japan, Korea, and Manchuria is a very similar tree to the English Yew but is more frost-hardy and not so large, usually less than 20 feet tall. It is not as commonly planted here as the English Yew. Horticultural forms vary from low and spreading to conical and upright columnar.

Leaves and fruit: The leaves are somewhat shorter, ½ to 1 inch, and more abruptly pointed, and the underside is marked by two broad bands of yellow or grayish pores. The spray of foliage is not flat, but the two ranks of leaves are pointed upward, forming a V. The succulent, berry-like red fruits with single seed are similar.

PODOCARPUS FAMILY (Podocarpaceae)
This family of four genera, absent from North America, is confined mostly to the southern hemisphere, although a few species are present in Japan and China. The genus *Podocarpus* is the only one of importance in cultivation in this region, and only two of its many species are in wide use.

Yew Podocarpus *(Podocarpus macrophylla)*
This tree, from Japan, is the species most often seen in cultivation as a graceful garden or tub specimen in shaded locations. Its foliage is weeping in habit. Since the tree is not frost-hardy it must be grown in sheltered locations.

Leaves and fruit: The entire, alternate, soft, flattened leaves are a bright glossy deep green above and paler beneath, 4 inches long by ½ inch wide, and spirally arranged on the drooping branches. Male and female flowers usually occur on separate trees. The fruit is a small greenish or purple cherry-like drupe with a single hard seed.

Fern Podocarpus *(Podocarpus gracilior* or *P. elongata)*
This is a graceful tree from South Africa which reaches a height of 50 to 60 feet in its native habitat, but is usually a small garden or tub specimen in this area. It is not frost-hardy, and does best near the coast and in protected situations. The tree responds well to pruning and shaping.

Leaves and fruit: The soft, bright green leaves, 3 inches long by ⅛ inch wide, tapering both to stem and tip, are spirally arranged on pendulous branchlets. The pendent sprays of foliage are willow-like in appearance. The fruit is a cherry-like purplish drupe about ⅓ inch in diameter.

PALMS AND THEIR ALLIES (Monocotyledons)
These trees have a single upright stem, or are sparingly branched, with very long parallel-veined leaves (linear, fanlike, or feather-like) at the apex or at the branch ends. The stem does not increase in diameter by annual rings, but irregularly, with fibro-vascular bundles distributed throughout a woody pith. Flower parts are usually in threes or sixes; seeds are flinty-hard, with a single seed leaf. Of the large and widely dispersed collection of trees in the tropics, a few are hardy enough to grow in central California.

Palm Family (Palmaceae)
Palm trees, with massive, long-stemmed leaves, either fan-shaped or feather-shaped, grow about a single terminal bud at the apex of the stem; the trunks are usually clothed with a "shag" of pendent dead leaves or roughened with their persistent leaf bases. Flowers are in long drooping clusters, ripening as a flinty-hard single seed, sometimes enclosed in a sweet

pulp. This very complex family includes some 200 genera and perhaps 4,000 species, mostly trees but some tropical vines and shrubs.

PALMS WITH FEATHER-SHAPED LEAVES
Canary Island Palm *(Phoenix canariensis)*

This palm from the Canary Islands, is said to have been brought to California by the Mission Fathers, and is more frequently seen than any other feather palm in this area. The massive trunk, 4 to 5 feet in diameter on old specimens, is usually roughened by the woody bases of old leaves. Although slow-growing,

Figure 10 Canary Island Palm

it reaches a height of 50 feet or more, with a crown diameter of 25 to 30 feet. Thus it needs plenty of room for adequate development. It is a striking tree for parks and large gardens. It is hardy and satisfactory throughout the region, but needs moderate irrigation in dry situations.

Leaves and fruit: The huge arching leaves, 15 to 20 feet long, form a rounded, feathery crown of decided beauty. The light green leaf segments, rising on each side of the heavy, spiny midrib, are folded upward, 12 to 16 inches long by 1 to 2 inches wide. The cream-colored flowers appear in long drooping clusters, with male and female flowers on different trees. On the female trees the branched flower stalks rise from boat-shaped spathes, and the small, datelike but inedible fruits, ½ to ¾ inch long, ripen as orange clusters in fall.

Senegal Date Palm *(Phoenix reclinata)*

This tree from Africa is a smaller but similar feather palm, distinguished by slender trunks which tend to occur in clumps of two or more by sprouting. The multiple stems make an attractive effect on sheltered lawns. Height is usually 25 feet or less, and diameter 12 to 18 inches. The trunk is ringed with the woody bases of old leaves. The tree is less hardy than the preceding species and needs a protected situation to do well.

Leaves and fruit: The 5- to 7-foot leaves are dark green, divided into spiny segments 12 inches long by 1 inch wide. They fold upward lengthwise and curve downward at their tips. Small yellowish flowers (male and female on separate trees) are borne in clusters on long drooping stalks in spring. Clusters of small, inedible datelike fruits appear in fall on female trees at the base of lower leaves. They are red-brown, ½ to ¾ inch long.

Wine Palm or Syrup Palm *(Jubaea chilensis* or *J. spectabilis)*

This tree from Chile is a feather palm which grows

to a height of 30 feet. The massive trunk, 3 to 5 feet in diameter, is much smoother than that of either of the preceding two species, and is marked only by leaf scars, without the persistent woody bases. Of moderate hardiness, it grows best in protected situations.

Leaves and fruit: The 6- to 10-foot leaves are erect or spreading, but few of them droop. The numerous segments are 1½ to 2 feet long and about an inch wide; the petioles are short and spineless. The flowers appear in panicles among the spreading leaves; male and female occur on the same tree. The globular yellow fruits are 1½ inches long; because they resemble little coconuts, the tree has been known as the Monkey Coconut.

Phoenix dactylifera, the Date Palm, so important in date orchards in the Coachella Valley, is rarely seen in this area.

PALMS WITH FAN-SHAPED LEAVES

Windmill Palm or **Fortune Palm** *(Trachycarpus fortunei)*

From central and eastern China comes the hardiest of all the palms locally cultivated. It is a small and daintily precise tree, 25 to 30 feet tall. The slender trunk is densely coated with hairlike fibers. It is a popular street and garden tree. The round display of foliage, about 10 feet across, gives it a windmill-like appearance.

Leaves and fruit: The leaf blades are 3 to 4 feet across, nearly round, with stems 2 to 3 feet long, slender to an inch wide, and blunt but not spiny points. The blades are divided about to the middle into many segments which are stiff and not drooping. Flowers are monoecious in clusters; the fruit is a dry, three-lobed, purplish drupe.

Figure 11 Windmill Palm (left)
Figure 12 Mexican Fan Palm (right)

California Fan Palm (*Washingtonia filifera*)

Native in the desert country of southern California, this palm has been extensively introduced throughout coastal and valley areas. Its massive trunk, averaging 3 feet in diameter, is carried with little taper from the swollen base to heights of 75 feet or more. The upper trunk is usually clothed with a dense shag of dead leaves which persist for many years. The tree is hardy throughout this area and gives a tropical aspect to much of the landscape.

Leaves and fruit: The huge fan-shaped bright

[47]

green leaves are borne in a tufted cluster at the top of the trunk surrounding the single large bud. The leaf blades are 3 to 6 feet broad, solid in the center but incised into many divisions which taper to slender, pendent tips. The margins of the divisions have many threadlike filaments. The leaf stalks are 3 to 5 feet long by 1 to 3 inches wide, and are armed with sharp hooked spines. Thus the globe-shaped crown may be 10 to 20 feet in diameter. Small creamy-white flowers appear in spring, clustered on branches of the 12-foot flower stalks; they look like corn tassels. The ovoid black fruits, ½ inch long, hang in dense clusters from the stalks. The hard seed is surrounded by a thin, sugary, edible pulp which was an item of food for the Indians.

Mexican Fan Palm (*Washingtonia robusta*)

From Mexico, as a young tree this is virtually indistinguishable from the preceding species, but it develops a much more slender trunk, reaches greater height, up to 100 feet, and, as the leaf stalks are shorter, the globe-shaped crown is somewhat smaller. The leaf segments have none or few marginal filaments; the leaf stalks are 2 to 3 feet long and armed with spines. The fruit is similar to that of the California Fan Palm.

Chinese Fan Palm or Fountain Palm (*Livistona chinensis*)

This palm from China grows to a height of 30 feet. The diameter of the trunk is 12 to 16 inches; it is relatively smooth, and marked by rings. There is a graceful crown of erect to spreading foliage. The tree is quite hardy in the Bay Region, and easily propagated, but is not so widely planted as the previous species.

Leaves and fruit: The shiny dark green leaf

[48]

Figure 13 California Fan Palm

blades, 3 to 5 feet long, are borne on leaf stalks as long as 7 feet, usually unarmed except at the base. The blades are cut to the middle into many segments which taper to a point and droop from a point about a foot from the tip. The leaves do not cling to the trunk to make a shag, as in the Washington palms, but stand out from the trunk at an angle until they fall. Small perfect flowers are borne in long-stemmed clusters, and ripen as clusters of ovoid, thin-fleshed black fruits.

Lily Family (Liliaceae)

Trees in this family have linear, pointed, and parallel-veined leathery dark green leaves borne in tufted clusters at the tips of a few spreading branches arising from a slender or sturdy trunk. White or cream-colored flowers of waxy consistency, three- to six-parted,

[49]

are borne in dense clusters on terminal spikes. *Yucca brevifolia*, the Joshua Tree, and other yuccas of the southwestern deserts belong to this family, but are rarely seen in cultivation here.

Green Dracena *(Cordyline australis)*

This species from New Zealand is a flat-topped tree, irregularly palmlike in appearance. It reaches a height of 40 feet with slender or stout trunk separating into about five spreading branches, each crowned with a tuft of leaves and terminal spikes of flowers. The Green Dracena stands heat, drought, and winds off the ocean, but not prolonged frost. It is often grown in tubs for tropical effect.

Leaves and fruit: The leathery, bladelike leaves, 20 to 36 inches long by 2 to 2½ inches wide, are borne in spreading rosettes at the branch ends. The fragrant, cup-shaped flowers are waxy-white and ripen as ¼-inch blue-white fruits.

Blue Dracena *(Cordyline indivisa)*

This is a smaller tree, also from New Zealand, and has much the same appearance as the Green Dracena, but is not quite so hardy and is usually found in sheltered gardens. It may become 20 to 25 feet tall, with a spread of the irregular crown to 15 feet.

Leaves and fruit: The leathery blue-green leaves are up to 6 feet long and 5 inches wide, with forty or more conspicuous veins on each side of the reddish midvein. White flowers are borne in dense drooping panicles as long as 4 feet and ripen as clustered small fruits.

Dragon Tree *(Dracaena draco)*

Native in the Canary Islands, this is a slender-trunked, rather grotesque tree with a few irregular branches, each with a tuft of linear leaves at the tip.

It may reach 50 or more feet in height, but is usually smaller. It resembles the Cordylines, to which it is closely related. It is drought- and wind-resistant, but will not stand severe frost. Some old specimens may be seen along streets, but it is now generally used sparingly as a novelty plant.

Leaves and fruit: The leathery glaucous green leaves are about 2 feet long by 1½ inches wide. They are swordlike, parallel-veined, and arranged in tufts at the tips of the branches. Numerous small greenish flowers occur in clusters on large terminal panicles, and ripen as globular orange-colored berries.

Abyssinian Banana(*Musa ensete*) is a monocotyledonous plant with light-green leaves, up to 20 feet long and 3 feet wide (usually much frayed by the wind). It can scarcely be considered a tree, although it may grow to a height of 15 feet or more. It is usually smaller, as it freezes down during many winters but sprouts again from the roots. It can be successfully grown only in very sheltered situations.

BROAD-LEAVED TREES;
HARDWOODS: DICOTYLEDONS

This large group of flowering plants includes trees of many families with leaves consisting of a simple or compound broad blade, usually on a stem or petiole, alternate or opposite in arrangement on the twigs, and usually having netted venation. Flowers are of many types, often showy and with flower parts in fours or fives, occasionally with male and female flowers on separate trees. Fruits of diverse forms enclose seeds in which the embryo usually has two seed leaves (cotyledons). The trees generally have spreading crowns of complex branching habit, and trunks which increase in diameter by annual growth of the cambium layer. The wood, usually of complex makeup, is strong and hard and takes a fine polish.

In tropical and semitropical regions, most of the tree species retain their leaves throughout the year and are classed as *Broadleaf Evergreens;* those growing in colder sections, which lose their leaves for the winter season, are known as *Deciduous Trees.* Both types are present in central California: broadleaf evergreens constitute a background of green foliage throughout the year; deciduous trees give the landscape touches of more rigorous climates when they turn color in the autumn and leaf out with soft green foliage in spring. Some in each group grow to large size, and a number are prized for their fine floral display. Those with evergreen foliage are better suited to the mild areas near the coast, and the deciduous species are more commonly planted inland. The two groups are treated separately, with the species grouped by families.

EVERGREEN BROADLEAF TREES

Broadleaf evergreens drop some leaves sparingly throughout the year and so maintain a green crown continuously. They are characteristic of mild climates and will not thrive in areas with prolonged freezing weather.

MYRTLE FAMILY (Myrtaceae)

The Myrtle family, with leathery, aromatic leaves, is especially numerous in Australia, where many large and important timber trees as well as beautiful ornamentals are included. The genera commonly seen here are *Eucalyptus, Eugenia, Leptospermum, Melaleuca, Metrosideros, Myrtus,* and *Tristania.* The Eucalypts are a host in themselves, with more than 500 species in Australia, ranging from 300-foot forest giants to desert mallees and subalpine shrubs. More than a

[52]

hundred species have been introduced experimentally since 1885, and about twenty-five have shown adaptability to conditions in this region; they constitute an important feature of the landscape, especially near the coast. A number of new and beautiful ornamental trees are now under trial.

Blue Gum (*Eucalyptus globulus*)

Native in Tasmania, this is one of the hardiest and most rapid growing of all Eucalypts. Brought to California more than a hundred years ago, it comprises about 80 percent of all the area planted to Eucalypts along the California coast, where it is especially valuable as a windbreak tree. On good soil Blue Gum groves grow at the rate of four to six cords of wood per acre per year. They reach heights of 200 feet, and their towering, cloudlike crowns give them great charm and beauty. The bark is shed in long strips, leaving the trunks smooth and with a tan and green color. The wood is used as a strengthening agent in fiber containers, and has been made into excellent hardboard products. The tree is well suited to coastal areas, but will not stand long exposure to temperatures below 20° F.

Leaves and fruit: The silvery-blue seedling and sprout leaves are rounded in shape, occurring opposite in pairs on square twigs. The mature leaves, deep green in color, are sickle-shaped, 6 inches long, alternate in arrangement on cylindrical twigs, and hang in vertical position on short leaf stalks. The fog drip from these pendent leaves adds much moisture in groves adjacent to the coast. The flower buds are blue-green, squarish in outline, about an inch in diameter, and crowned with a warty operculum or cap. They are borne singly in the leaf axils. When the cap falls off, as it does in all Eucalypts, cream-colored stamens spread in a rosette surrounding a slightly de-

[53]

pressed nectar cup with the erect pistil in the center. There are no petals. The ripe fruit is a four-parted, hard woody capsule an inch in diameter; the valves

Figure 14 Blue Gum

open to release small black seeds embedded in tan-colored chaff. In favorable situations the tree reseeds itself well.

The dwarf and much-branched variety *compacta*, known as Bushy Blue Gum, has been extensively planted along the state highways in the Bay area, and as a low windbreak. It retains the blue foliage for several years. Two species closely allied to Blue Gum are now being planted: Maiden's Gum (*E. maideni*), and Eurabbie (*E. bicostata*). Both have smaller and clustered fruits, but similar seedling and mature leaves.

River Red Gum (*Eucalyptus camaldulensis* or
  E. rostrata)

This has the most extensive distribution of any Eucalypt in Australia, mostly on bottomland along streams. Somewhat more frost-hardy and drought-resistant than Blue Gum, it is the species most commonly seen in the Sacramento and San Joaquin valleys. The bole is usually crooked and the crown irregular and spreading even in plantations. Many trees have a weeping habit, with the lower branches sweeping the ground in pendent sprays. The trunk bark is smooth with a mottled tan and green appearance. The reddish heartwood is more durable in the ground than that of Blue Gum.

Leaves and fruit: Red Gum leaves are shorter, narrower, and less sickle-shaped than those of Blue Gum, and the cylindrical twigs are dark red. The buds, flowers, and fruits are small (¼ inch), borne in stalked umbels usually numbering seven, but varying from five to fifteen. The buds are sharply beaked, and in mature fruits the capsule valves protrude beyond the rim. Tiny tan-colored seeds are indistinguishable from the associated chaff.

Forest Red Gum or **Gray Gum** (*Eucalyptus tereticornis*
  or *E. umbellata*)

This is a taller and more erect tree of better form, with ascending branches and a less spreading habit of growth. Some trees are very similar to Red Gum, and it seems likely that there are hybrid forms. The tree stands heat and drought very well and is about as frost-hardy as Red Gum.

Leaves and fruit: The leaves are somewhat broader than those of Red Gum, especially in the young foliage; the bud and fruit clusters are in stalked umbels of slightly larger size; the caps or opercula are conical and not beaked. The seeds are virtually the same in appearance.

Moitch or Desert Gum (*Eucalyptus rudis*)

This is another very similar tree with leathery blue-green foliage and upright habit of growth; the lower stem is clothed with a thin, fibrous, netted bark. It survives desert heat with some irrigation, but also makes good growth on low-lying windy areas around San Francisco Bay, where it is commonly used along the state highway.

Leaves and fruit: Flowers are white, as in the preceding two species, and the bud and fruit clusters are similar but somewhat larger, and the conical caps usually turn white before they fall to release the rosette of anthers. There are probably hybrid or intermediate forms of these three species.

Manna Gum (*Eucalyptus viminalis*)

This tree is one of the hardiest and most beautiful of the Eucalypts grown in California. It becomes a stately tree with smooth white bark and cloudlike masses of ribbony foliage. It has demonstrated excellent resistance to frost.

Leaves and fruit: The leathery bright green leaves are long and narrow and hang in ribbony clusters. Buds, flowers, and fruits occur in short-stalked clusters of three in the shape of a cross. Caps are dome-shaped, and the globular ripened fruits are about ¼ inch in diameter. The flowers are white or light cream-colored.

Scarlet Gum (*Eucalyptus ficifolia*)

This is the most striking ornamental of all Eucalypts in local cultivation. It is a small tree with dense rounded crown and fibrous, furrowed brownish bark on the short trunk. It is not frost-hardy in areas back from the coast.

Figure 15 Scarlet Gum

Leaves and fruit: The ovate, leathery dark green leaves are 5 inches long, paler green beneath and bronze-colored when young. The flame-red to pink blooms occur in terminal clusters of great brilliance and beauty, sometimes almost covering the crown. The best displays are usually in February and March and again in July and August. The smooth woody capsules, about the size of smoking-pipe bowls, hang in heavy, stalked clusters during much of the year, gradually changing color from green to brown. The seeds are large and winged.

Red Ironbark or **Mugga** *(Eucalyptus sideroxylon)*

From New South Wales comes one of the most frost-hardy species here. It becomes a tall, erect tree with somewhat weeping foliage, furrowed bark, dark brown to black, marked by shiny crystals of kino. In Australia the tree produces heavy and durable construction timbers. It is growing well in highway plantings from north of Corning to Selma; the most popular type is a pink-flowered variety *rosea*.

Leaves and fruit: The long-stalked leaves are 3 to 5 inches long and half as wide, gray-green or bluish-green on both surfaces, and tapered to a blunt point. Buds, flowers, and fruits are borne in stalked clusters of three to five from the axils of the leaves. The short cone-shaped caps fall to permit unfolding of the rosettes of white, pink, or deep red stamens. The goblet-shaped red-brown fruits are borne in pendent arrangement, and have valves deeply enclosed in the cup.

Narrow-leaved Ironbark *(Eucalyptus crebra)*
This is similar to the Red Ironbark in appearance, but the leaves are narrower, the furrowed bark is not so dark in color, and the tiny buds, flowers, and fruits are borne in multiple clusters. It is also a frost-hardy and dependable species for valley conditions.

Red Box or Round-leaved Eucalyptus *(Eucalyptus polyanthemos)*
This is a hardy and desirable street and highway tree with slender, upright form. The mottled bark is not shed in strips but remains smooth, becoming fibrous and persistent on the base of older trees. Growing slowly to moderate size and thriving under various conditions, this ornamental tree is popularly called "Dollar" Eucalyptus.

Leaves and fruit: The gray-green leaves are rounded or oval, with a slight notch at the apex. They form a rather open and somewhat weeping crown. Tiny white flowers, borne in great profusion in pendent terminal clusters, ripen into attractive panicles of small urn-shaped capsules.

Yellow Box or Honey Eucalyptus *(Eucalyptus melliodora)*
This is similar to the preceding species, but has a

somewhat denser crown, spreading and upright, and roughened persistent bark.

Leaves and fruit: The slender, taper-pointed gray-green leaves, 4 to 5 inches long, form graceful sprays of foliage. The small buds, white or pink flowers, and fruits occur in terminal umbel clusters. It is noted as the best honey tree of all the Eucalypts, and should increase in popularity in this region.

Silver-leaved Gum or Corkscrew Gum *(Eucalyptus pulverulenta)*

A small subalpine tree in Australia, this is now being widely planted in California for the beauty of its foliage, which is popular for use in floral displays. It is a small and frost-hardy tree of irregular spreading habit which is usually cut back to induce production of the foliage.

Leaves and fruit: The round silvery-gray leaves, about the size of silver dollars, are borne in corkscrew arrangement on the young twigs. Mature leaves are more slender and pointed, but are rarely seen. White flowers are borne in three-flowered umbels in the axils of the leaves. The fruits are ⅓ inch across.

Several other Eucalypts with rounded, glaucous juvenile foliage are being grown as desirable garden ornamentals. These include *E. gunnii, E. cordata, E. urnigera, E. kruseana, E. coccifera, E. perriniana,* and *E. cinerea.* Species with very narrow leaves and attractive willow-like form are *E. nicholi, E. linearis, E. salicifolia,* and *E. spathulata.*

Swamp Messmate *(Eucalyptus robusta)*

This species is a tree of coastal tidal flats and sandy areas in New South Wales and Queensland, with an erect habit of growth and thick, fibrous red-brown bark. It makes good growth in low-lying areas around San Francisco Bay, but will not stand much frost. It produces very large crops of flowers and fruits when but a young tree.

Leaves and fruit: The leathery dark green leaves are lighter green beneath, alternate in arrangement, stalked, and from 4 to 8 inches long by 1½ to 3 inches wide. The venation is fine and almost parallel, making an angle of 50 to 60° with the midrib. The buds, ½ to ¾ inch long by less than ½ inch wide, grow on definite stalks up to ½ inch long. Flowers are borne in umbels of seven or more in the axils of the leaves on flattened, strap-shaped peduncles. The cap is drawn out into a long point and falls to release the cream-colored stamens. Fruits are cylindrical to vase-shaped, ½ inch long or more by ¼ inch wide. The valves are short and pointed, about at rim level.

Eucalyptus resinifera, a larger, but similar tree, from the same coastal region in Australia, is occasionally planted here. It has smaller and globe-shaped fruits in stalked umbels and narrower and more pointed leaves. It stands shady situations very well and grows on better soils than the preceding species, but is not very frost-hardy.

Other Eucalypts being planted in some quantity include: the large trees *E. obliqua, E. cornuta, E. leucoxylon, E. diversicolor, E. botryoides,* and *E. cladocalyx;* and the smaller sized *E. platypus, E. lehmanni, E. torquata,* and *E. caesia.* Many drought-resistant mallees are worthy of trial planting.

Australian Bush Cherry *(Eugenia myrtifolia* or *Syzygium paniculatum)*

This species has been known for many years by the name *Eugenia myrtifolia.* It is an attractive columnar tree with glossy green foliage tinged with reddish-bronze when young. Although usually of moderate size, it grows rapidly on good soils and in protected locations near the coast, and may reach 50 feet in height. It is subject to damage by frost, heat, or severe winds.

Figure 16 Australian Bush Cherry

Leaves and fruit: The simple, shiny dark green leaves, 2½ to 4½ inches long, are opposite in arrangement, with entire margins, and occur on somewhat pendent branchlets. White flowers about ½ inch across are borne in dense, feathery clusters in early summer, and sometimes nearly hide the foliage. The shiny purple fruits, ¾ inch long, are borne in clusters in early winter. They have a bland subacid taste and are sometimes used in making jelly.

Cajeput or Punk Tree, Paper-bark Bottle-Brush
(*Melaleuca leucadendra*)

This is one of a number of trees and shrubs from Australia which bear flowers arranged around the stems with long stamens, giving the twig a resemblance to a bottle-brush. It is an upright tree, up to 40 feet tall, with pendulous branches of shiny foliage. The spongy tan trunk bark is very unusual; it sheds in thin papery layers, giving the bole a punky appearance. The tree will stand poor soil, brackish areas near the coast, ocean winds, and heat, but is not frost-hardy.

Leaves and fruit: The shiny gray-green leaves

have a reddish tinge when young. They are simple, alternate, and parallel-veined, with entire margins, 2 to 4 inches long and about ¾ inch wide, tapered both to stem and tip. Showy white flowers are arranged around the twigs, their long stamens giving a bottle-brush appearance. The cup-shaped brownish capsules, 3/16 inch wide, surround the stem in clusters 2 to 3 inches long, and persist for a year or more.

Several other species of *Melaleuca* are planted near the coast and in sheltered situations. All have similar clustered flowers with long stamens united at the bases into five groups, and dome-shaped woody fruits surrounding the stems. Most have shorter and more linear leaves, and some have pink or lilac flowers. The species may be *M. styphelioides* (flowers white), *M. nesophila* (flowers pink), *M. ericifolia* (soft, linear leaves and yellowish-white flowers), and *M. armillaris* (branchlets drooping, flowers white).

Trees and shrubs of the genus *Callistemon* are very similar in leaf, flower, and fruit, and are also called Bottle-brush. In these, however, the stamens are single instead of grouped in fives.

Brilliant Bottle-brush *(Callistemon citrinus* or
  C. lanceolatus)

Also called Lemon Bottle-brush, this is a small tree to 30 feet tall, widely planted for its clustered brilliant red flowers. The lanceolate leaves, 1 to 2½ inches long by ¼ inch broad, are dark green and shiny on both surfaces, tapering to a sharp point; the midrib and two lateral veins are prominent. The flowers have 1-inch stamens. The ovoid capsules are contracted at the outer edge.

Callistemon brachyandrus is a similar tall shrub with stiff, narrower leaves to 1½ inches long, the flowers with dark red stamens and yellow anthers. It makes an attractive small street tree.

Callistemon viminalis (*C. speciosus*), called the Showy Bottle-brush or Fire-fall Tree, with its dense bright-red flower clusters and weeping habit, is a popular species which may reach a height of 40 feet. The lanceolate leaves are 1½ to 4 inches long and ¼ inch broad, with entire margins and rounded or sharp tips. They are light green and glossy, with prominent midrib but more obscure lateral veins. The flower clusters enclose 2 to 4 inches of stem, and the globular capsules are not contracted above.

Other bottlebrushes commonly in cultivation here include *C. salignus,* the Willow Bottle-brush (yellow or pink flowers); *C. violaceeus* (narrow leaves, lavender flowers); and *C. linearis* (linear leaves to 5 inches, spikes of red flowers).

Australian Tea Tree *(Leptospermum laevigatum)*

This is another Australian tree with a number of horticultural forms which may grow to a height of 25 feet, but is usually crooked and shrubby, with a characteristic bark which shreds away in strips. The tree will stand poor, sandy soils, and the tough leathery foliage persists in windy situations along the coast.

Leaves and fruit: The shiny, myrtle-like, entire gray-green leaves are ½ to 1 inch long and display three prominent veins. The little white flowers, with rounded petals and many stamens borne in great profusion on short stalks, look like pinwheels against the dark green foliage. The capsular woody fruit is cup-shaped, about ¼ inch across, and has eight to ten cells.

Manuka Tea Tree *(Leptospermum scoparium)*

This tree from Australia and New Zealand has a number of showy horticultural forms and is a somewhat smaller tree, 18 to 25 feet, but often in dwarf types. The leaves are narrow and ½ inch long, silky when young and quite variable. Flowers are red, pink, or white. Red-flowered forms are very popular, and have such names as Double Rose, Red Sparkler, Fairy Rose, and Ruby Glow. The fruits are small, dome-shaped, clustered capsules.

Brush Box (*Tristania conferta*)

This large tree from the coastal areas of New South Wales and Queensland reaches a height of 140 feet. The bole, 3 to 6 feet in diameter, is clothed at the base with fibrous, somewhat scaly light-gray bark. The smooth reddish bark of young trees is an attractive feature. The foliage and habit of growth resemble those of Scarlet Gum. Though the main range is below 2,000 feet, it does grow in valleys to an altitude of 3,000 feet, where it withstands ten to twenty-five frosts per year.

Leaves and fruit: The broad, leathery, glossy, dark green leaves are 4 to 6 inches long, opposite when young and clustered at the tips of the twigs when older. Young shoots are hairy and the resting buds are scaly. The star-shaped white flowers, 1½ inches across, with many stamens, bloom in small clusters in the leaf axils. They ripen as stalked, bell-shaped, smooth, three-celled capsules, with three blunt enclosed valves; the cells contain a few angular wedge-shaped seeds about ½ inch in diameter.

Smooth-barked or Brown Apple (*Angophora costata* or *A. lanceolata*)

This tree from Queensland and New South Wales is an attractive tree with pendent sprays of foliage. It reaches a height of 80 feet and a trunk diameter of 1½ to 3 feet. The bark is shed in oval plates, leaving a smooth pink or orange surface with slight depressions; it often shows stains from kino gum. It is

[64]

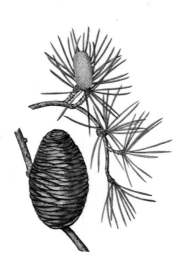

Deodar Cedar

Japanese Black Pine

Italian Stone Pine

Aleppo Pine

Plate 1

Oriental Arborvitae

Moitch or Desert Gum

Scarlet Gum

Red Ironbark or Mugga

Plate 2

Loquat

Cork Oak

Kurrajong Bottle Tree

English Walnut

Plate 5

Weeping Willow

Lombardy Poplar

European White Birch

English Elm

Plate 6

Common Fig

Tulip Tree or Yellow Poplar

Flowering Plum

Kwanzan Cherry

Plate 7

Pink Double Hawthorne

Eley Crabapple

Black Locust

Silk Tree or Mimosa

Plate 8

quite hardy in its native country, standing summer heat to 100° F. and forty to fifty frosty nights a year. It is a nice ornamental tree in the vicinity of Sydney. In California it grows well in mild coastal areas to 1,000 feet elevation.

Leaves and fruit: The juvenile leaves are light green, entire, opposite in arrangement on short stalks or sessile on the slender twigs. The mature leaves are deep green; they retain the opposite arrangement, are stalked, 2 to 5 inches long by 1 inch or less in width, and taper to a blunt point. The venation is parallel and regular from a prominent midrib at an angle of about 75°. The cream-colored flowers occur as three-flowered groups in terminal clusters. They ripen as stalked, vertically ribbed capsules about ½ inch long with thin rims and three to four cells containing broad flat seeds.

Other small trees of the Myrtle Family occasionally grown in sheltered gardens include: *Feijoa sellowiana,* the Pineapple Guava; *Psidium guajava,* the Lemon Guava; *Psidium cattleianum,* the Strawberry Guava; and *Metrosideros excelsa* (*M. tomentosa*), the New Zealand Christmas Tree.

BEAN OR PEA FAMILY (Leguminosae)

This very large family, of worldwide distribution, has many genera and hundreds of species, including both broadleaf evergreen and deciduous trees, mostly with compound leaves. It is variable in flowers and foliage, but normally the hard seeds are borne in a pod.

The acacias, from Australia and South Africa, are a large and very ornamental genus, mostly with fern-like compound leaves and golden yellow to cream-colored flowers which are commonly planted in this area. They do best along the coast, as some frost injury occurs inland. In some the leaves are reduced to broad leathery stems, or phyllodes, with entire margins and parallel veins. Many species are shrubs.

Green Wattle *(Acacia decurrens)*

This tree and its two varieties, the Silver Wattle (*A. decurrens* var. *dealbata*), and the Black Wattle, (*A. decurrens* var. *mollis*), are similar in habit of growth and appearance. They grow rapidly to heights of 30 or more feet, with spreading crowns, but are short-lived, and apt to lose branches in windstorms. All have feathery compound foliage, masses of golden-yellow flowers in spring, flat pods in fall, and smooth gray-green bark as young trees. The bark is an important source of tannin in some parts of the world. Silver Wattle has the most glaucous foliage and is most frost-hardy.

Figure 17 Silver Wattle

Leaves and fruit: The feathery double compound leaves are composed of tiny ¼-inch leaflets arranged in parallel rows. The leaves are alternate in arrangement, 4 to 6 inches long, gray-green or silvery and decorative in appearance. The fragrant golden flowers are borne in early spring as tiny fuzzy balls in drooping, branched clusters in the axils of the leaves. The racemes, 12 to 14 inches long, virtually cover the entire crown (Feb. to Mar.) and are popular for flower arrangements. They ripen as flat red-brown pods, 2 to 4 inches long by ¼ inch wide, containing hard

[66]

black seeds, and persist on the tree for several months. The trees spread by natural seeding in some areas.

Bailey Acacia or **Cootamundra Wattle** *(Acacia baileyana)*
This is a smaller, flat-topped spreading tree up to 30 feet tall, with attractive blue-gray or purplish foliage of the same type as the preceding species, and has similar golden flowers in dense pendent racemes. It grows rapidly and has a fine display of foliage and flowers, but is not long-lived and is apt to break badly in windy situations, especially when in full bloom (Jan. to Mar.) It does well in sheltered gardens not far from the coast, but is not frost-hardy.

Blackwood Acacia or **Sally Wattle** *(Acacia melanoxylon)*
This tree is native along the southeastern Australian coast from Brisbane and Tasmania to Adelaide on a variety of soils from near sea level to 3,500 feet elevation, where there may be up to seventy frosts a year. The hardiest of the acacias, it may reach 100 feet in height and 4 feet in diameter, but is usually smaller. It has a spreading crown and dark brown bark. It produces a fine ornamental timber for cabinet and decorative work, but the supply is limited. In central California, where it has been planted for many years, it is a fast-growing and hardy species which responds well to pruning, but has a wide-spreading root system. It is one of the dependable trees used along the state highway system, but will not stand severe frost.
Leaves and fruit: The dark green foliage consists of broad, flat, simple, leathery leaf stalks (phyllodes), 3 to 5 inches long by 1 inch wide, in alternate arrangement. Young shoots often show the phyllode supporting a double compound leaf with fifteen to twenty pairs of leaflets, ½ by 1/10 inch on each pinna, which

decrease in size toward the tip. The mature leaves are curved, lanceolate, and blunt-pointed, but taper toward the base. There are three to five longitudinal veins with finer net veins between them, and a small gland marks the upper edge of the phyllode near the base. The branchlets are somewhat angular. The flowers are borne in tan-colored heads on axillary racemes ½ to 1 inch long, with thirty to fifty flowers to the raceme. Fruit is a twisted and contorted flat brown pod, 2 to 6 inches long by ¼ to ½ inch wide, bearing six to ten oval or disc-shaped black seeds, to ¼ inch long, encircled by a doubly folded bright-red appendage.

Other acacias with phyllode foliage which are commonly used for erosion control, sand-dune planting, and hedge or garden planting include *A. longifolia*, the Sydney Golden Wattle; *A. retinodes*, the Everblooming Acacia; *A. cultriformis*, the Knife-blade Acacia; and *A. cyclops*, a shrubby light green type now used along highways. Other species may be found in sheltered special collections.

Carob or **St. John's Bread** *(Ceratonia siliqua)*
This, from the Mediterranean region, is the desert tree with plump, sweet, mealy pods reputed to be the food on which St. John was able to survive in the wilderness. It grows slowly, but is long-lived, and old specimens may reach a height of 30 to 40 feet with about an equal crown diameter. The compact, rounded crown of dense, shiny foliage stands heat and drought, but not much frost. It is successfully used as a street tree in mild areas, but has succumbed to occasional severe frosts in inland valley areas.

Leaves and fruit: The compound leaves, 6 to 9 inches long, consist of six to ten oval, leathery, entire leaflets borne opposite in pairs along a slender rachis. The leaflets, 2 to 3 inches long, are dark green and shiny above, and lighter green beneath. Male and female flowers are on different trees, appearing in spring as small yellowish blossoms from red buds. The plump, shiny brown pods ripen on female trees in fall. They are thick and leathery, 6 to 12 inches long by 1½ inches wide, with very hard, plump brown seeds. The pods are edible, sweet and mealy, with sugar content up to 40 percent and rich in protein. Pod production is rare in central California, and the trees grow well only in sheltered and nearly frost-free situations.

Laurel Family (Lauraceae)

The Laurel Family comprises trees and shrubs with simple, alternate, usually aromatic foliage, small flowers, and drupe or berry-like single-seeded fruits. The native California Laurel belongs in this family.

Grecian Laurel or Bay *(Laurus nobilis)*

This was a favorite of the ancient Greek poets, to whom it was a symbol of achievement. Olympic and other victors were crowned with laurel wreaths. The tree closely resembles the native California Laurel, and its aromatic leaves are used as flavor in cookery. It grows slowly to a height of 40 to 50 feet, with a handsome, rounded dense crown, but is often used in patios or as a tub specimen.

Leaves and fruit: The leathery, shiny, dark green leaves are 2 to 4 inches long by 1½ inches wide, with entire margins, and taper both to stem and tip. They are alternately arranged on short petioles. When crushed they have a pleasant fragrance, less pungent than that of the California Laurel. The fruits are purplish-black berries, ½ inch in diameter, with a single seed in a soft pulp, about half the size of those of the native tree.

Camphor Tree *(Cinnamomum camphora)*

This tree from China and Japan is one of the most

widely used street and ornamental trees throughout this area. The broadly rounded crown of foliage is beautiful throughout the year. Growth is slow, but the tree may reach 40 or more feet in height. It adapts to many soils, stands heat and some alkali, and is fairly frost-hardy.

Leaves and fruit: The glossy light green leaves show attractive tints of reddish-bronze when new growth is developing and some reddish tones are in evidence during much of the year. The leaves, 3 to 4½ inches long by 1 to 2 inches wide, in alternate arrangement on short petioles, give off a strong camphor fragrance when crushed. Tiny yellow flowers are borne in clusters shorter than the leaves, and ripen as clustered, beadlike black berries about ⅜ inches in diameter, set in a shallow cup.

Avocado (*Persea americana*)

This tree, from Central America, is extensively grown in southern California orchards for the large edible fruits, of which there are a number of named varieties. The tree grows easily from the large seed and is commonly seen as a garden ornamental here, though it does not often produce edible fruit. On deep, fertile soils and in sheltered locations it becomes a large tree with a dense crown. It is not suitable for frosty situations. The first Avocado tree in this region was received as a gift from Guatemala and planted beside Strawberry Creek in Berkeley in 1879. It has grown to moderate size.

Leaves and fruit: The leaves are glossy dark green above, paler green beneath, 5 to 10 inches long by 3 to 4 inches wide, in alternate arrangemen' on stout greenish twigs. The margins are entire. The pear-shaped fruits are 4 to 6 inches long, with a greenish to purplish sometimes warty skin and edible green pulp surrounding a large seed.

Bellota Tree *(Cryptocarya miersii)*

This tree from Chile is occasionally planted and grows to be a fine spreading ornamental up to 50 feet in height. A well-grown specimen can be seen on the north bank of Strawberry Creek south of Agriculture Hall on the Berkeley campus of the University of California.

Leaves and fruit: The thin, shiny, leathery leaves are about 2 inches long by 1 inch wide, opposite in arrangement, with entire, wavy margins. They have short petioles and prominent veins beneath. Small thin-fleshed oval fruits, about the size of olives, develop from tiny bisexual flowers borne in panicles. Another species, *C. rubra,* also from Chile, has smaller leaves which are glaucous beneath; otherwise it is similar.

CASHEW FAMILY (Anacardiaceae)

The Cashew Family is composed of trees and shrubs with leathery compound or simple leaves, resinous bark, bisexual or unisexual flowers, and nutlike or berrylike fruits. Some species yield varnish materials or medicinal products. The genus *Rhus* includes several shrubs of wide distribution in California, of which *R. diversiloba,* Poison Oak, is most cordially detested. The fruits of cashew, mango, and pistache are edible, but not grown here.

California Pepper or **Peruvian Mastic** *(Schinus molle)*

This tree from South America is a familiar sight throughout much of the coastal and valley areas in California. Mature trees may reach 50 feet in height with an equal spread of crown. The sturdy gnarled trunk, clothed with fibrous red-brown bark, supports a rounded crown of fernlike foliage on gracefully pendent branchlets which often sweep the ground. It grows rapidly and is resistant to heat and drought,

[71]

but may be injured by sharp frosts in exposed locations. Because of the shallow and wide-spreading root system, it needs plenty of room; it should be well-watered when young and may require spraying to control scale insects. There are many fine old and picturesque trees throughout our area.

Leaves and fruit: The feathery alternate light green leaves are 6 to 12 inches long, composed of twenty to sixty shiny leaflets 1 to 2 inches long by ¼ inch wide, with entire or sparingly toothed margins and tapered to a slender point. The small, yellowish flowers are in pendent clusters, mostly in early summer. Male and female flowers are on different trees. The female tree bears quantities of ¼-inch rose-colored berries in attractive drooping clusters.

Brazilian Pepper *(Schinus terebinthefolius)*

This is a much smaller tree, 25 to 30 feet tall, which is a good street and garden tree in mild areas near the coast, but is less frost-hardy than the California Pepper. It has an erect habit of growth and forms a rounded crown resembling that of carob, with which it is sometimes planted on streets. It grows rapidly and is quite free from pests, usually requiring little attention.

Leaves and fruit: The compound leaves are alternate in arrangement, 6 to 8 inches long, composed of seven leaflets borne opposite on a slender, winged rachis. Leaflets are 1 to 2 inches long and less than an inch wide, shiny dark green above and paler beneath, with entire or sparingly toothed margins. The small white flowers grow in clusters, with male and female on different trees. The female tree produces bright red berries in terminal clusters 2 to 3 inches long; the showy berries are about ⅛ inch in diameter.

Cabrera or **Tree Pepper** *(Schinus polygamus* or
S. *dependens)*

This is a smaller and much hardier tree from South America now being tested as a street tree throughout California. It stands heat, drought, and some frost, has a nice upright form with spiny branches, and grows quite rapidly to a height of about 15 feet.

Leaves and fruit: The leaves are small, simple, leathery, and oblong in shape, with entire margins, and occur in alternate arrangement on the spiny twigs. Small clustered yellow flowers ripen on female trees as deep purple berries in pendent racemes.

PITTOSPORUM FAMILY (Pittosporaceae)

This rather large family of evergreen trees and shrubs has simple alternate leaves, five-parted, often fragrant flowers, and pulpy, berry-like, or capsular fruits. The name refers to the seed being embedded in a pitchy, resinous substance which is aromatic and bitter. Many species are native in Australia and New Zealand; those planted here are similar in leaves and fruit.

Orange Pittosporum *(Pittosporum undulatum)*

The Orange Pittosporum, or Victorian Box, from Australia, is extensively used in hedges and shrubbery and as single trees for its glossy foliage and clusters of fragrant flowers. It develops into a slender round-headed tree up to 40 feet or more tall. It is the largest species of Pittosporum, and on good sites may reach 60 feet. The bark is smooth and dark gray. It is hardy in dry and windy areas and along the coast, but does not stand much frost.

Leaves and fruit: The glossy light green leaves are alternate in arrangement on the slender twigs, 3 to 5 inches long by 1½ inches wide, tapering to both

[73]

ends with entire, wavy margins. Older leaves are darker green and somewhat less wavy. The cream-colored,

Figure 18 Orange Pittosporum

five-parted flowers, ½ inch across, occur in dense clusters about 3 inches wide. The blooming period is about six months, and the heavy orange-blossom fragrance is attractive to bees. The clustered fruits, ½ inch across, split open when ripe to display many small seeds embedded in orange-colored jelly.

Other *Pittosporum* species in common use here include the following: *P. eugenioides,* Tarata, from New Zealand, to 30 feet tall, yellowish-green leaves 2½ to 4 inches long with wavy margins, leaf midrib often whitish, greenish-yellow flowers ¼ inch long in terminal clusters; *P. tenuifolium,* Tawhiwhi, from New Zealand, 6 to 25 feet tall, dark brown stems, black bark, thin, oval dark green leaves with undulate margins, clustered flowers, dull purple, black, or rarely yellow; *P. rhombifolium,* Queensland Pittosporum, 30 to 50 feet tall, diamond-shaped leaves 2½ to 4 inches long with toothed margins, clustered white flowers, persistent shiny yellow to orange capsules, somewhat less frost-hardy than the others, more common south;

P. phillyraeoides, Willow Pittosporum, graceful, willow-like tree to 30 feet, narrow, entire spiny-tipped leaves on pendent branchlets, yellow flowers, ⅜ inch solitary in leaf axils, yellow capsules ½ inch long; *P. crassifolium,* Karo, from New Zealand, 20 to 25 feet tall, leaves 2 to 3 inches long, dark green and shiny above, white tomentose beneath on pubescent branchlets, flowers ½ inch long, almost black, in terminal clusters, capsules pubescent, ¾ to 1¼ inches long, used for windbreaks and hedges.

Protea Family (Proteaceae)

The Protea Family includes southern hemisphere trees and shrubs abundant in Australia and South Africa. Some yield edible nuts or dye-stuffs. *Macadamia ternifolia,* the Queensland Nut, of Australia, and *Leucodendron argenteum,* the striking Silver Tree of South Africa, are occasionally seen in sheltered situations here, along with spiny or leathery-leaved shrubs of the genus *Hakea,* used in hedges. *Hakea laurina,* the Sea Urchin, is a shrub or small tree grown for the beauty of its leathery foliage and bright red flowers.

Silk Oak *(Grevillea robusta)*

This becomes a large forest tree in Australia, with wood resembling that of the oak. It is narrow-crowned, with spreading branches bearing feathery, fernlike foliage. The root system is shallow and wide-spreading. The tree grows rapidly, is hardy to drought and frost, and makes a good street and highway tree and background planting in parks.

Flowers and fruit: The graceful, twice-compound fernlike leaves are 6 to 12 inches long; the irregularly shaped leaflets, mostly lobed, have rolled edges. They are dark green above and silvery beneath.

[75]

Slender bright orange flowers occur in summer in sprays 2 to 4 inches long. The fruit is a woody brown pod containing one or two flat winged seeds.

Magnolia Family (Magnoliaceae)

The tree members of this family usually have good form, showy tulip-like flowers, large leaves, and hardwood of high quality for cabinet work. Some are called cucumber trees from the shape of the multiple fruit clusters.

Southern Magnolia or Bull Bay (*Magnolia grandiflora*)

This tree, from the southeastern United States, is notable for its dense crown of glossy foliage and its striking display of large white flowers. In the south it is a valuable timber species up to 100 feet tall, but in this region it usually grows to only half that height. There are many fine old specimens throughout this region. Since improved clones are being developed at Saratoga, it should become a more popular species for street planting in the future.

Leaves and fruit: The shiny, leathery dark green leaves are 7 to 8 inches long by 2 to 3 inches wide with wavy, entire margins. They are smooth above and more or less coated with rusty hairs beneath. The large waxy-white flowers are 6 to 10 inches across, with six petals forming a broad cup. They have a pleasing fragrance and bloom over a long period. They mature as stalked, cucumber-shaped, multiple fruits, 3 to 4 inches long and half as wide, pinkish in color and finely hairy. The mature fruit is brown, and the capsules open to display plump bright red seeds.

Staff-Tree Family (Celastraceae)

This family includes a widely distributed number of trees and shrubs, both evergreens and deciduous, including *Euonymus*, Burning Bush; *Celastrus*, Bittersweet vine; and the native low shrub *Pachystema*.

Mayten Tree *(Maytenus boaria)*

This tree, from Chile, is a slow-growing, graceful tree with dainty sprays of pendulous foliage resembling the weeping willow, but with shorter leaves. It rarely exceeds 30 feet in height, and the rounded crown is 10 to 20 feet across. It is an attractive small tree for streets and gardens, and does well in interior valleys with irrigation, but is sensitive to prolonged frosty periods. The tree often develops multiple trunks, but responds well to pruning. Its dainty and delicate appearance belies its real hardiness. There are eight fine trees about forty years old on the Quad at the Davis campus of the University of California.

Leaves and fruit: The smooth, thin light green leaves are 1 to 2 inches long by ½ inch wide, with finely toothed margins. They are alternate in arrangement, tapering both to stem and tip. Small greenish-white blossoms appear in clusters in the leaf axils in early summer and ripen as small pealike scarlet capsules.

MULBERRY FAMILY (Moraceae)

Trees in the Mulberry Family have alternate, simple leaves and tiny unisexual flowers in heads or clusters, or enclosed in a receptacle as in *Ficus*. They are mostly deciduous, except for the figs, which are widely distributed in tropical areas, and range from very large trees to trailing vines.

Moreton Bay Fig *(Ficus macrophylla)*

This fig, from Australia, grows to a massive tree with buttressed trunk and wide-spreading branches. The tree reaches a height of 50 to 60 feet, with a much broader spread of branches on old specimens. It does best in areas near the coast, as it will not stand many degrees of frost. There are good specimens on both sides of San Francisco Bay, but massive specimens are seen farther south. In Australia it is used as an avenue tree, but here its use is limited to parks and large estates. The heavy, wide-spreading root system is a problem except where plenty of room is available.

Leaves and fruit: The simple dark green leaves, shiny above and brownish beneath, are alternate in arrangement, 6 to 10 inches long by 3 to 4 inches wide, on petioles about an inch long. They are leathery, with entire margins, and clothe the smooth branches so thickly as to give dense shade. Tiny flowers occur within a globe-shaped receptacle which ripens as a small inedible fig, ¾ to 1 inch in diameter, spotted with white.

Indian Laurel Fig *(Ficus retusa)*

This fig, and its variety *nitida*, from India and Malaya, is now being extensively planted in milder areas as a street and ornamental tree. It is fast-growing, from 30 to 40 feet tall, with an erect habit of growth and rounded crown of dense foliage. It responds well to pruning, does well on a variety of soils, and makes a nice small tree even on narrow parkways. However, it is not hardy in areas with frosts below about 20°F.

Leaves and fruit: The entire dark green leaves are 2 to 4 inches long and half as wide. The reddish or orange-colored fruits are ⅓ inch long, with blunt basal bracts.

HOLLY FAMILY (Aquifoliaceae)

The family includes three genera of trees and shrubs with simple, alternate leaves, often dioecious, and berry-like red fruits with hard seeds. The Yerba Mate, *Ilex paraguariensis*, is an important beverage plant in South America. Many varieties of holly are used as ornamentals and for production of the attractive foliage and berries for Christmas decorations.

English Holly (*Ilex aquifolium*)

This is a small tree from Europe with a number of varietal forms which does best on good soil and in cool areas along the coast. It grows slowly in gardens and occasional plantations, up to a height of 30 feet or more, but needs irrigation on dry soils. While frost-hardy, it does not thrive in areas of high temperature. The tree responds well to pruning and has few pests.

Leaves and fruit: The simple, alternate, leathery leaves are 2 to 3 inches long and half as wide, shiny deep green, sometimes variegated, and usually with wavy margins armed with sharp prickles. The tiny fragrant white flowers ripen as clusters of bright red berries, ⅓ inch in diameter, on wood of the previous year. Male trees produce no berries, but are needed to provide pollen for the female flowers. This may be accomplished by grafting.

Chinese Holly (*Ilex cornuta*)

This is a smaller tree from Asia, also with a number of horticultural forms, which is much better adapted to heat and drought conditions of the interior valleys. Usually shrubby to about 10 feet tall, it spreads by root suckers to form clumps. The glossy bright green leaves are 3 inches long, quadrangular in outline, with strong spines and a three-pointed apex. The clustered plump berries are more orange-red than in the preceding species.

Several other hollies are in cultivation, especially *I. crenata* from Japan with many horticultural forms, and *I. opaca*, from the eastern United States, are sometimes cultivated.

HEATH FAMILY (Ericaceae)

The large and widely distributed Heath Family, mostly woody shrubs, includes Scotch Heather and the varied manzanita species of California brush fields. Many have tiny, bell-like cream-colored flowers in clusters. The tubular flowers of rhododendrons, azaleas, Kalmias, and Arbutus are fine ornamentals. Salal of the north Pacific Coast, wintergreen of New England, and the huckleberries, bilberries, and cranberries produce edible fruit.

Strawberry Tree (*Arbutus unedo*)

This tree from the Mediterranean region is closely allied to the native Pacific Madrone, but is rarely more than 15 feet tall. It is commonly grown here for its dense foliage, showy clustered fruits, and smooth reddish bark which sheds in thin plates from trunk and branches. It is frost-hardy to about 15° F., and on good soil may reach a height of 30 feet.

Leaves and fruit: The leaves, 4 inches long and half as wide, with serrate margins, closely resemble those of the native toyon, and have a bitter, astringent taste. They are shiny dark green above and paler beneath, tapering to the base. The bell-shaped white flowers occur in drooping panicles in summer and ripen as multiple red fruits about the size, shape, and color of strawberries. The fruits, while edible, are usually flat and rather tasteless.

OLIVE FAMILY (Oleaceae)

This large and widely distributed family includes twenty genera and about 400 species, and is especially abundant in the East Indies and East Asia. The trees have opposite, simple or compound leaves, rather inconspicuous clusters of flowers, and variable fruits. Syringa and jasmine are favorite ornamentals. The olive has been cultivated for centuries for its edible fruit and oil. The ashes include excellent hardwood timber trees and the privets are popular street trees and hedge and ornamental shrubs.

Common or **Mission Olive** *(Olea europaea)*

From the Mediterranean region, this is listed as one of the ten most useful trees of the world, and has produced edible oil and fruits for thousands of years. It is an important orchard tree in California, and also a fine ornamental, hardy and drought-resistant. It grows slowly to a height of about 25 feet and its moderate size makes it desirable for planting on streets and highways and as a garden ornamental. It lives to a great age and often has a much gnarled and irregular trunk with smooth gray bark. It withstands desert heat with some irrigation, and is frost-resistant in valley and foothill areas.

Leaves and fruit: The slender, leathery gray-green leaves, silvery on the under side, are 2 to 2½ inches long, opposite in arrangement, tapering toward the base. Margins are entire. Tiny white flowers occur in drooping clusters in such profusion as to give the entire crown a feathery white appearance. The fruits are shiny purple-black drupes with a succulent mesocarp surrounding a hard seed. The fruits constitute a problem when they fall on sidewalks.

Glossy Privet *(Ligustrum lucidium)*

From China and Japan, this is a tall shrub or small tree up to 30 feet tall; the dense rounded crown of upright branches is sometimes 20 feet across. It grows easily on a variety of soils, stands much heat and some frost, and can be pruned to shape. It makes a good street tree. There are a number of horticultural forms, some variegated.

Leaves and fruit: The simple, glossy, leathery leaves have short stalks and entire margins, and are opposite in arrangement. They are 4 to 6 inches long, tapering from a rounded base to a slender tip, and usually fold upward from the midrib in a trough shape. Small fragrant white flowers occur in dense,

[81]

erect, pyramidal spikes up to 10 inches long in summer. The fruits are clustered, ¼-inch black berries in fall.

The California Privet (*Ligustrum ovalifolium*) from Japan, and the Common or English Privet (*L. vulgare*) from the Mediterranean are both widely used in formal hedges and shrubberies. They have shorter leaves, up to 2½ inches long, and each has a number of ornamental forms. While usually small, they occasionally grow to 15 feet or more in height.

Shamel or Evergreen Ash *(Fraxinus uhdei)*

This tree from Mexico has been introduced quite recently. It grows rapidly and apparently thrives in this region, although most specimens are still of small size. It has an open crown of foliage and opposite branching habit, and resembles the deciduous ash tree in appearance.

Leaves and fruit: The large light green leaves are pinnately compound, opposite in arrangement, and consist of five to nine stalked, shiny leaflets on a central stalk. The stout, smooth-barked gray-green twigs terminate in a dome-shaped bud. The inconspicuous male and female flowers are borne on separate trees in dense clusters. Symmetrically winged, "canoe-paddle" fruits occur in pendent clusters on female trees.

ROSE FAMILY (Rosaceae)

This large and complex family, with about 1,500 species distributed throughout the world, includes many of the finest fruit and ornamental trees and shrubs. Typically the flower parts are in fours or fives, with showy petals; the fruit is a berry, drupe, or pome. Many of the trees and shrubs are deciduous and some have spiny branchlets. The following evergreen species are commonly introduced in this region.

Loquat (*Eriobotrya japonica*)

This tree from China and Japan grows to a height of 25 to 30 feet with an irregular, spreading crown of dense, large-leaved foliage. It thrives on a variety of soils, is rarely injured by heat or frost, stands pruning, and with irrigation and care produces edible fruit.

Leaves and fruit: The leathery, deep green leaves, 10 to 12 inches long by 2 to 4 inches wide, are simple and short stalked; the margins are shallowly dentate, with a heavy vein running from midrib to each tooth. They are shiny above and coated with rusty hairs beneath. The small, fragrant white flowers, ¼ inch across, occur in pendent clusters in fall and winter, but are almost embedded in the densely hairy stems. Pear-shaped orange-yellow fruits, 1 to 3 inches long, ripen in late spring in clusters of three to ten. They are edible, with a pleasantly acid pulp in which several plump seeds are embedded.

Chinese Photinia (*Photinia serrulata*)

This tree from China is allied to the native toyon, but has much larger foliage and may become 30 or more feet tall.

Leaves and fruit: The glossy leaves are 5 to 7 inches long by about 2 inches wide, on 1-inch leaf stalks. They are shiny on both surfaces and have wavy, coarsely toothed margins. The leaves, toned with bronze when they unfold in spring, become dark green above and lighter green beneath for most of the year, but some of them turn scarlet in fall. The red color may be encouraged by occasional pruning to induce new leaves to form. The densely clustered white flowers ripen in the fall as red berries, ¼ inch in diameter, which are less brilliant than the native Christmas Berry.

Carolina Cherry (*Prunus caroliniana*)

From the southeastern United States, sometimes known as Wild Orange, Mock Orange, or American Cherry Laurel, this tree is now being planted as a desirable small evergreen street tree in this region. It grows well under varied conditions, is frost-hardy, stands pruning well, and eventually becomes a tree 30 feet or more tall.

Leaves and fruit: The thin, shiny dark green leaves are 2 to 4 inches long and half as wide, with entire margins and short petioles, and are tapered to the tip. The tiny white flowers, borne in racemes 1½ inches long, ripen as glossy black cherries ½ inch in diameter. Many of these persist on the tree throughout the winter. The leaves are shorter and narrower, with less acuminate margins than the following evergreen cherries.

Cherry Laurel or **English Laurel** (*Prunus laurocerasus*)

This tree from Europe is extensively planted as a hedge and for the fragrance of its flowers, but under favorable conditions it may become 20 feet tall with a fine display of glossy foliage. It is usually kept to smaller size by pruning.

Leaves and fruit: The thick leathery leaves, with entire or finely serrulate margins, are 2½ to 6 inches long and about half as wide, obovate in shape with a short petiole, and marked by two to four glands near the base of the blade. They are shiny dark green above and paler beneath. The fragrant white flowers, about ⅓ inch across, occur in dense racemes which are *shorter* than the leaves—2½ to 5 inches. The dark purple cherries, about ½ inch long, ripen in drooping clusters in late summer.

Portugal Laurel (*Prunus lusitanica*)

This tree from Spain and Portugal is similar to the preceding species, but usually has somewhat darker and less glossy foliage. In good sites it grows to a height of 35 feet, but is usually pruned to smaller size, and normally produces multiple stems.

Leaves and fruit: The leathery leaves are ovate in shape, with finely toothed margins and petioles ½ to 1 inch long. They are dark green above and paler beneath, 2½ to 4 inches long by about half as wide, and alternate in arrangement. Small white flowers, about ¼ inch across, are borne in showy spikes 5 to 10 inches long—*longer* than the leaves, and often in such profusion as to transform the tree into a white cloud. The ¼-inch purple-black cherries are borne in pendent clusters in late summer.

Catalina Cherry or Lyon Cherry (*Prunus lyonii*)

This tree from the Santa Barbara Channel Islands has been introduced on the mainland. It grows to be a handsome tree, up to 35 feet tall, with dense glossy foliage, attractive flower clusters, and large fruit. It is often used in ornamental plantings with the native Islay or Hollyleaf Cherry, which it closely resembles. Apparently there are hybrid forms between the Islay and the Catalina Cherry.

Leaves and fruit: The leathery dark green leaves,

Figure 19 Catalina Cherry

3 to 5 inches long by 1½ inches wide, taper from a rounded base to a blunt apex. The leaf margins are mainly entire and longer than those of Islay. The small white flowers are borne in dense racemes 2 to 4½ inches long, a few of which ripen as plump cherries an inch in diameter, purple-black in color, with thin flesh and a very large seed.

Catalina or Island Ironwood (Lyonothamnus floribundus var. asplenifolius)

Another introduction from the Santa Barbara Channel Islands, this does well in areas not far removed from the coast, but does not thrive in hot or frosty areas. It grows to a broad-crowned tree 50 feet tall or more, with interesting fernlike foliage and a sturdy trunk with fibrous red-brown bark which peels off in long vertical strips. The outer bark weathers to an attractive silvery-gray color. Unless controlled by pruning, the tree may develop multiple stems.

Leaves and fruit: The leaves are opposite in arrangement and of two kinds. In the species, most of the leaves are simple, bladelike, and leathery, with virtually entire margins 4 to 6 inches long by ¼ inch wide. In the variety, the leaves are compound and fernlike, composed of three to eight leaflets which are deeply cut to the midrib into triangular segments. They are dark green above and lighter green beneath. The small, white flowers, ¼ inch across, bloom in dense flat-topped clusters in midsummer. They are loosely branched and 4 to 8 inches across. The clustered fruits are ¼-inch woody capsules ripening in fall, containing four hard oblong seeds, usually with poor germinative capacity.

Soapbark Tree (Quillaja saponaria)

From Chile, this grows slowly to form a large spreading tree with an open crown of shining foliage and dark furrowed bark containing saponin. It somewhat resembles the live oaks in habit of growth, and reaches a height of 60 feet. One large tree is at the Center Street entrance to the Berkeley campus of the University of California, and there are several smaller specimens near the buildings.

Leaves and fruit: The thick, leathery, stalked leaves are ovate in shape, about 1½ inches long, with wavy or shallowly dentate margins. They are light green and shiny on both surfaces. The small white flowers, about ¼ inch across, are borne singly or in terminal clusters of three to five. These ripen as dry, leathery, persistent fruits consisting of five carpels containing many small seeds.

Evergreen Pear *(Pyrus kawakamii)*

This is a recent introduction from Japan which is achieving popularity for its hardiness, attractive evergreen foliage, and pleasing display of clustered flowers. It will stand temperatures to about 18° F., and develops into a tree 15 or more feet tall. It will evidently make a good street and ornamental tree, and is sometimes trained in espalier form.

Leaves and fruit: The leathery light green leaves are 4 to 5 inches long, with a broad blade on a long petiole, wedge-shaped at the base and tapered to a blunt point. They are glossy on both surfaces and have wavy and sometimes finely toothed margins. Typical five-parted single white flowers are borne in spring, but do not often mature to fruits here.

BEECH-OAK FAMILY (Fagaceae)

This widely distributed family of woody plants, with simple, alternate leaves and acorn or nut fruits, numbering about 600 species, includes some of the most useful timber trees of the world. Although most of them are deciduous, there are evergreen species of *Castanopsis, Lithocarpus,* and *Quercus,* with native California trees in each of these genera.

Cork Oak *(Quercus suber)*

This tree from the Mediterranean region closely resembles the native Coast Live Oak in habit of growth and general appearance, except for the soft, fluted light-gray bark which is the source of commercial cork, an important product of the cork oak stands in Portugal and Spain. It can be stripped at intervals of ten to twenty years without injury to the tree, and is exported in large quantities from these countries. Cork suitable for ground cork products has been stripped from California trees, but commercial production is not economically feasible. Cork oaks have been planted in this state for more than a hundred years, and many fine trees are to be seen, the largest a 60-inch diameter veteran, 100 feet tall, at Napa State Hospital in Napa County. Excellent ornamental trees surround the Quad on the Davis campus of the University of California, and grow also in Lakeside Park in Oakland.

Leaves and fruit: The oval leaves are 1½ to 3 inches long and half as wide, bright green and glossy above, and prominently veined and grayish on the underside. They occur on short petioles with remotely toothed margins, sometimes nearly entire, and are alternate in arrangement. Flowers are of two kinds, borne on wood of the current year: the female on short green stalks; the male on threadlike, wispy pendent catkins which dry and fall soon after shedding the pollen. Plump green to brown acorns, 1 to 1½ inches long, embedded in a fringed cup having stout, recurved scales, ripen the first autumn. They average 60 to 75 per pound.

Holly Oak or **Holm Oak** *(Quercus ilex)*

This tree is also from southern Europe, where it

grows in association with Cork Oak, which it closely resembles in growth habit and foliage, except for the bark, which is dark, hard, and furrowed. This fine, erect round-headed tree, with sturdy branches and glossy foliage, is increasingly popular as a street and ornamental tree.

Leaves and fruit: The leaves are variable in shape, short-stalked, 1½ to 2 inches long and half as wide, very dark green and glossy above and silvery-pubescent beneath. The margins may be remotely toothed and holly-like, but some are entire with a slightly rolled edge. The flowers are similar to those of the Cork Oak, being of two kinds borne on the wood of the current year, the female maturing as brown acorns ¾ to 1¼ inches long, set about half their length in a top-shaped cup with flat thin scales.

Both of these introduced live oaks are subject to attack by the caterpillars of the California Oak Moth, and may require prompt spraying to prevent defoliation.

BEEFWOOD FAMILY (Casuarinaceae)

This family with a single genus is native in Australia and the Pacific Islands. The tree is sometimes known as the Australian Pine because of the slender needle-like twigs, and the name Beefwood comes from the blood-red color of the heartwood. The slender, jointed foliage is said to resemble the feathers of the casso-wary. Leaves are reduced to tiny scales at the joints of the slender green stems. The globular fruits are made up of many beaked capsules, and resemble cones in appearance. Three species are commonly planted here.

Beefwood or **River She Oak** *(Casuarina cunning-hamiana)*

From Australia, this is a hardy and fast-growing tree up to 70 feet tall. It is able to survive saline conditions along the coast and some alkalinity in valley areas, and makes a good windbreak. The open conical crown gives it a pinelike appearance, but the jointed twigs show that it is not a pine. The deep red heartwood is hard and durable and is called "oak" in Australia. The largest trees of this species that I have seen are in Livermore. Most trees of this family are now believed to be of this species, and not *C. equisetifolia*.

Leaves and fruit: The leafless, jointed, slender pale green twigs function as leaves; the leaves are reduced to tiny scales at the joints, in this species six to eight. The flowers are inconspicuous, with male and female flowers on different trees: the male in slender terminal spikes; the female in small heads in the axils of the twigs. The conelike globular fruits are woody and brown, ½ inch in diameter, with pubescence on the valves.

She Oak or Beefwood *(Casuarina stricta)*

This is a smaller tree, 10 to 30 feet tall, with spreading crown and pendent foliage. The internodes are longer than in the preceding species, ½ to 1 inch long. There are normally ten tiny scalelike teeth at each node. The globular woody fruits are from ¾ to 1¼ inches long and ovoid in shape. It is a good ornamental tree, more drought-hardy than the preceding species.

STERCULEA FAMILY (Sterculiaceae)

This family of alternate-leaved plants, mostly tropical, has five-part bisexual flowers and capsular fruits. The commercial products chocolate, cocoa, and cola nut are supplied by members of this family. Our native *Fremontia californica* of the foothill country belongs here.

Kurrajong Bottle Tree (*Brachychiton populneum*)

This is one of several Australian bottle trees with smooth bark on a somewhat swollen trunk resembling a bottle. It has a fine, rounded crown of glossy foliage, grows slowly to a height of 50 feet or more, and is widely used in mild areas as a street tree. It will stand heat and drought, but not much frost.

Leaves and fruit: The glossy green leaves, 2 to 3 inches long and half as wide, vary in outline from entire to three-lobed blades on slender petioles. The terminal clusters of bell-shaped white flowers with red spots inside are an attractive feature. They ripen as clustered woody brown pods 2 to 3 inches long, containing large plump seeds. After splitting open, the pods appear like little canoes in shape. They persist on the tree well into the winter.

TAMARISK FAMILY (Tamaricaceae)

About 100 species in four or five genera of small trees and shrubs are distributed from the Mediterranean region to Japan. The heathlike alternate leaves, persistent petals from the small flowers, single-celled ovary, and bearded seeds are characteristic. Many are heat- and alkali-resistant, and are therefore extensively used for desert windbreaks in areas where the climate is not too cold.

Athel or **Desert Tamarisk** (*Tamarix aphylla*)

This is the largest of the genus, growing to a height of 30 or more feet. It has an irregular habit of growth, with masses of feathery foliage. It is remarkable for its ability to tolerate heat, poor soil, alkali, and saline conditions near the sea. Easily propagated from branch cuttings, it is usually seen as a windbreak or tall hedge. It responds well to pruning, and suffers from breakage if branches are permitted to become too long. The shallow, wide-spreading roots require root pruning where the tree is used as a windbreak in irrigated orchard areas. Although it sometimes freezes down in valley areas, it sprouts vigorously from the roots and recovers rapidly. Some other shrubby specimens of *Tamarix* with pendent spikes of flowers are grown as ornamentals in gardens.

Leaves and fruit: The gray-green leaves are very small and overlap the slender twigs, with only the tiny points free. They persist for more than a year. In the jointed green twigs it somewhat resembles the *Casuarina* species, but the leaves are more numerous and the flowers are more showy. The very small, sessile pink flowers appear in summer in erect terminal panicles. The fruit is a dry capsule containing many small seeds, each with an apical tuft of hairs.

Rue Family (Rutaceae)

The Rue Family, of about 100 genera of trees and shrubs, is widely distributed in regions of mild climate. It has variable leaves, flowers with three to five sepals and petals, and the same or double the number of stamens. The fruits are of various forms, some pulpy and edible, the best known of which are the orange and allied citrus fruits. Only the hardier citrus varieties will thrive here, as most are not tolerant of frost.

White Sapote (*Casimiroa edulis*)

This tree from Central America is occasionally grown in southern California, but will not stand temperatures below 20° F. It grows to a height of 30 to 50 feet, with alternate, palmately compound light-green leaves, with three to seven stalked leaflets, and bears globular, thin-skinned green fruits about 3 inches in diameter on long stems. The edible pulp, containing three or four seeds, tastes like that of a peach.

Sweet Orange *(Citrus sinensis)*

This tree from China is of great economic importance as an orchard tree in areas of mild climate. When well grown it is 15 to 20 feet tall, with a rounded crown of dense foliage, sturdy trunk, and branches which bear occasional blunt thorns. It is usually damaged by temperatures below 20° F., and thrives only in sheltered situations in this area. Orchardists growing this and other citrus fruits are generally prepared to use orchard heaters when temperatures drop much below 29° F., and the Weather Bureau gives warning of impending frosty periods. A number of horticultural and orchard varieties of orange trees, including dwarf forms, are grown as ornamentals in sheltered gardens throughout this area, and some of them produce very good fruit. This is true also of some varieties of Lemon, *C. limon,* especially the dwarf variety known as the Meyer Lemon. The Valencia variety of orange is a favorite ornamental tree, for both flowers and fruits are on the tree during much of the year.

Leaves and fruits: The glossy deep green leaves are alternate in arrangement, oval in shape with entire margins and leathery texture; they are 3 to 5 inches long and about half as wide, and have a slightly winged leaf stalk. The clustered waxy-white flowers have the well-known heavy fragrance. The globular fruits are 3 to 4½ inches in diameter, with wrinkled, deep orange-colored skin and sweetly acid pulp in which plump seeds are embedded except in the navel varieties. Grapefruit (*C. paradisi*), lime (*C. aurantifolia*), and other varieties are usually grown successfully only in areas virtually free from frost. They are very similar to the orange in habit of growth, size, foliage, and general appearance.

Wilga *(Geijera parviflora)*
This is a small to medium-sized tree from Australia

with a rounded crown of graceful foliage somewhat resembling the willow. It has wide distribution on the plains of western New South Wales, where it is considered a desirable ornamental. In Australia some of the foliage is eaten by sheep, which avoid that of nearby trees that appear to be botanically the same. In its native area the tree has rough dark-colored bark on the trunk and smoother and lighter-colored bark on the branches.

Leaves and fruit: The leathery leaves, 3 to 6 inches long by less than ½ inch wide, are borne in pendent position which gives the tree an attractive willow-like appearance. Small white or cream-colored flowers are borne in short, wide, pyramid-shaped terminal clusters. The egg-shaped fruits, ¼ inch long, contain a single shiny black seed.

DECIDUOUS BROADLEAF TREES

These trees drop all their foliage for at least a part of each year, usually in the cooler winter months, although there is some variability, and a few species which are evergreen in warmer climates are deciduous here. Some put forth leaves early in spring and drop them in early fall; others are later in leafing out and retain their foliage much later in autumn. Deciduous trees are sometimes overlooked in this region because of the wealth of broadleaf evergreens, but they really outnumber the others, including more than sixty species in twenty-two families from many parts of the world. Even with little frost many of them add distinctive color to the autumn landscape, and some put on fine flower displays before the leaves in spring. They include tall and stately park and avenue trees; some are excellent street trees of moderate size, and others produce both showy flowers and edible fruits. The oaks, maples, hickories, and walnuts include some of the finest hardwood timber trees of the world.

WALNUT FAMILY (Juglandaceae)

The Walnut Family includes trees with pinnate compound leaves, male flowers in pendent catkins, and fruits which are hardshelled edible nuts or winged nutlets in drooping racemes. They comprise some of the finest timber, ornamental, and orchard trees of the world. The hickories have twigs with solid pith, whereas in the walnuts the pith is chambered. The genera used here are *Carya, Juglans,* and *Pterocarya.*

English Walnut or Persian Walnut *(Juglans regia)*

This tree, native from the Mediterranean region to China, is broad-crowned with smooth gray bark on sturdy branches. It may reach a height of 60 feet or more, but is usually kept shorter by pruning. It is of great economic importance in this region as an orchard tree for the production of edible walnuts, and there are several named varieties for this purpose. The best walnut crops are produced on sandy-loam soil with good care and summer irrigation. The named varieties are grafted on rootstocks of the native Hinds Walnut, which shows the dark and furrowed bark of the black walnut below the point of union. It is in wide use as a street, park, and garden tree throughout this region. Large trees in the Mediterranean region and Asia Minor produce the finely figured "Circassian" Walnut so highly prized for furniture and cabinet work.

Leaves and fruit: The compound bright green leaves, 10 to 16 inches long, are alternately arranged on stout, smooth twigs which show naked greenish buds in winter. The sessile leaflets are opposite in pairs, 2 to 4 inches long by 1½ inches wide, oval in shape with entire margins. The tiny male flowers are borne in early spring on pendent, wormlike catkins. The inconspicuous green female flowers, on short stalks, develop into globular green fruit about 2 inches in diameter; its thick husk splits after maturing to release the nearly smooth, thin-shelled, light tan nut.

American Black Walnut (*Juglans nigra*)

This is a tall and stately forest tree with dark and furrowed trunk bark from the eastern United States. It is characteristic of fertile soils throughout much of the middle-western and eastern forest region, where large trees produce probably the most valuable hardwood timber of any American tree. It closely resembles the native Hinds Walnut, from which it differs in greater size, longer leaves, and the deeply sculptured shell of the nut. It requires a good soil and adequate summer irrigation to do well here.

Leaves and fruit: The compound leaves, 12 to 24 inches long, with pubescent petioles, have from fifteen to twenty-three lanceolate leaflets 3 to 3½ inches long and half as wide, with serrate margins above the middle; the terminal leaflet may be small or often missing. They are glossy green above and finely pubescent beneath. The globular green fruits are 2 inches in diameter, with a slightly roughened skin and thick pulp containing a powerful brown stain, which dries almost black in color; the fruits do not split to release the nut. The hard shell of the nut is deeply furrowed into sharp ridges.

Butternut (*Juglans cinerea*)

This tree of the eastern United States is only occassionally seen here. Its wood is a lighter brown than than of the Black Walnut, but it has a pleasing grain and figure. The bark, which is more brownish, shows a few smooth plates; the leaves have eleven to seventeen leaflets of about the same size and shape as those of the preceding species, but are pubescent on both surfaces as well as on the central stalk. Fruit is narrower and longer, up to 2½ inches long; the outer skin is coated with a sticky reddish pubescence. The slender ovoid nut is even more deeply and sharply ridged than in the Black Walnut, and the kernel is somewhat more oily.

Since walnut trees hybridize rather commonly, many show intermediate characteristics between the parents. Some grow rapidly to be fine large trees with valuable figured wood. The hybrids among *J. nigra, J. hindsii,* and *J. cinerea* are known as Royal hybrids; those having *J. regia* as one of the parents are termed Paradox hybrids. Some especially beautiful figured wood from the Paradox cross has been sold in the lumber trade as the "Claro Walnut" and has brought fancy prices. It is said that such trees probably originate from nuts borne by a *J. hindsii* or *J. nigra* tree growing in an area surrounded by an orchard of *J. regia* trees.

Pecan *(Carya illinoensis* or *C. illinoinensis)*

This tree, from the eastern and southern United States, is tall, sturdy and broad-crowned with deeply furrowed dark brown bark, massive branches, and attractive foliage. The stout smooth-barked twigs have solid pith and large scaly terminal buds. Selected varieties produce the thin-shelled pecan nuts of commerce throughout the southern states, but in California the tree is usually seen as an ornamental, rarely in orchard form. The tree shows excellent adaptability for growing in the interior valleys, and there are good street and ornamental trees in Sacramento, Chico, Merced, Dos Palos, Fresno, and other valley towns.

Leaves and fruit: The compound leaves, 15 to 18 inches long, are alternate in arrangement. The eleven to fifteen asymmetrical (sickle-like) light green leaflets, 5 to 7 inches long by 1½ to 3 inches wide, are sessile or very short-stalked, with finely toothed margins. The leaflets, which turn golden yellow in autumn, resemble those of walnut, but differ in the sickle shape. Inconspicuous bisexual flowers occur on the same tree in spring, and ripen as ovoid fruits 2 to 2½ inches long, with a thin husk which splits open to release the oval, pointed brown nut with a thin smooth shell.

The Shagbark Hickory (*Carya ovata*) and the Big Shellbark or King-nut Hickory (*C. laciniosa*) are occasionally seen here. They both have rough, shaggy bark, compound leaves with five to seven broader leaflets with serrate margins, and four-angled nuts with flinty hard light tan to white shells borne in fruits with thick husks.

Chinese Wingnut *(Pterocarya stenoptera)*
From China and northern Persia, this develops into a broad-crowned tree 30 to 50 feet tall, with a fine crown of compound foliage and interesting drooping panicles of fruits. It often develops multiple stems. The tree stands poor soil and heat, but needs moisture during the dry season. When young it may be damaged by frost.

Leaves and fruit: The alternate, pinnately compound leaves are 8 to 12 inches long, consisting of eleven to twenty-three oval leaflets, 2 to 4 inches long and half as wide, borne in alternate arrangement on a winged rachis or leaf stem. The leaflets are bright shiny green above, paler beneath, and have finely toothed margins. The tiny flowers in pendent clusters ripen as attractive racemes of clustered nutlets, each fitted with double, pointed leafy wings. They turn brown and hang on the tree after the leaves fall.

PLANE TREE OR SYCAMORE FAMILY (Platanaceae)
A single genus, *Platanus*, of five species makes up this family of tall, spreading streamside trees with smooth mottled bark, broad-bladed and deeply lobed leaves, and multiple fruits in globular heads on pendent stems. They grow rapidly, respond well to prun-

ing, and are widely used for street and highway planting in many countries, but are subject to defoliation by the sycamore canker disease, *Gnomonia veneta*, which can be controlled by consistent spraying.

London Plane *(Platanus* x *acerifolia)*
A hybrid between *P. occidentalis*, of the eastern United States, and *P. orientalis*, of the Mediterranean region, this is in wide use as a street tree throughout our area. It grows rapidly, has a dense crown of large leaves, and a sturdy frame of branches with smooth, mottled bark. It responds well to pruning to size and form. On good sites, if unpruned, it may reach a height of 100 feet, but is usually kept to smaller size by pruning to a flat head of short, knobby branches. It is not as subject to sycamore canker as is the native sycamore, but spraying is often necessary. Other sycamores, except the native *P. racemosa*, are rarely seen in this area.

Leaves and fruit: The large, broadly lobed leaves occur in alternate arrangement on stout petioles which expand at the base to enclose the conical buds completely, thus hiding them until the leaves fall. The leaf blades are flattened or heart-shaped at the base, 6 to 10 inches wide, three- to five-lobed, with coarse teeth on the lobes (rarely entire), dark green above and lighter beneath, finely hairy when young but smooth later. The tiny flowers are borne in densely clustered globular heads which ripen as two or three bristly globular balls on a pendent stalk. The fruit heads, 1 inch in diameter, hang on the tree after the leaves fall until winds break them up to release the small winged seeds.

WILLOW FAMILY (Salicaceae)
This family, comprising the willows and poplars, is of wide distribution throughout the northern hemis-

phere. Both species include rapid-growing but often short-lived trees and shrubs with simple, alternate leaves, light-weight wood, bitter bark, and catkin-like flower clusters with male and female on different trees. Tiny seeds are wind-borne on cottony wings, for which many of the poplars are called cottonwoods. Willows usually have narrowly lanceolate leaves on short petioles with leafy stipules at the base, and finely serrate margins; the plump buds are enclosed by a single bud scale. Poplars have broad leaf blades on long cylindrical or flattened petioles, with serrate or dentate leaf margins; the winter buds, with several bud scales, are sometimes coated with resinous balsam. Poplars tend to be tall, upright trees, whereas willows are spreading or scrubby, with multiple stems. Both occur naturally on bottomlands and along streams and grow easily from cuttings. Of the many species, relatively few are cultivated.

Weeping Willow (*Salix babylonica*)

This tree from China is widely planted in this and other regions for its broadly rounded crown of gracefully weeping branches. It is fast-growing, attains a height of 40 feet or more, requires consistent soil moisture, and does well on irrigated lawns.

Leaves and fruit: The narrow, lanceolate, finely-toothed light green leaves often persist on the smooth olive-colored twigs to midwinter. Flowers are in catkins on different trees; the female ripens to release tiny seeds with cottony white wings. The cultivated variety "Crispa," the Curl-leaf Willow, is somewhat more open-crowned, and the slender gray-green leaves are curled in the shape of a ring. Of the many species of willow, this is about the only one often seen in cultivation, although some exotic willows have escaped from cultivation and grow along streams. *Salix discolor*, from the eastern United States, and S. *pur-*

purea, from Asia, are shrubby types cultivated in gardens as pussy willows.

Figure 20 Weeping Willow

White Poplar or **Abele** *(Populus alba)*

From Europe and Asia, this is often a small spreading tree with irregular form, but there are tall upright forms, notably (cult. var.) "Bolleana," (*Pyramidalis*). The white to gray-white bark is marked by darker patches, and the smooth greenish-white branches have twigs and buds coated with white hairs. Since many sprouts arise from the wide-spreading, shallow root system, the trees often occur in clumps. The wood is brittle, and branches are subject to breakage in high winds. This species and the succeeding one have been used in the development of fast-growing hybrid poplar strains in Spain and Italy.

Leaves and fruit: The simple, lobed leaves are 3 to 5 inches long including the stout petiole, alternate in arrangement, shiny dark green above and coated beneath with silvery hairs. They are coarsely toothed and so maple-like in shape that the tree is often mistaken for the Silver Maple. Male and female flowers are borne in drooping catkins on different trees. The female flowers release small cottony-winged seeds when mature. The male catkins fall soon after releasing the pollen.

Common Cottonwood *(Populus deltoides)*

From the middle west and the Mississippi Valley, this becomes a large tree, up to 90 feet in height, with a spreading crown. It has been planted widely throughout the United States as a fast-growing tree for quick effects. Such planting is now being increased on bottomlands in the Gulf states for the production of paper pulp; the trees are propagated by cuttings. Those of large girth are cut for lumber. There are undoubtedly hybrids with the Valley Cottonwood and other species of *Populus*.

Leaves and fruit: Typical leaves are 7 inches long, delta-shaped or slightly rounded at the base, shiny green above and lighter beneath, with toothed margins and long stalks. Female trees bear masses of cottony winged seeds which become a problem, so most ornamental poplars are grown from cuttings taken from male trees.

Lombardy Poplar *(Populus nigra* cult. var. "Italica"

This well-known tree of the western Asia and Mediterranean regions is an erect, columnar tree with ascending branches and is commonly used in windbreaks, background planting, or as an accent tree in gardens or parks. It grows rapidly under a variety of conditions, reaching a height of 60 feet or more, and is one of the most widely planted trees over much of the world. It is not long-lived, but is hardy and attractive to about forty years. This selected clone of the European Black Poplar is propagated by cuttings from male trees and so does not produce seeds or "cotton." The root system of this and other poplars is shallow and invasive, and the root sprouts are troublesome in lawns.

Figure 21 Lombardy Poplar

Leaves: The leaf blades, 2 to 4 inches long by 2 to 3 inches wide, are broadly wedge-shaped at the base, or sometimes nearly diamond-shaped. They have finely toothed margins and are borne on flattened petioles 1½ to 3 inches long in alternate arrangement. Like many other poplars the golden-yellow fall coloration is a notable feature.

Several other poplars are occasionally cultivated, including *P. simonii*, from China, with obovate dark green leaves; *P.* x *canadensis*, the hybrid Carolina Poplar; and the native *P. fremontii*, Fremont or Valley Cottonwood. There are probably many hybrid trees in cultivation. The aspens from the north and high mountains are rarely cultivated.

Birch Family (Betulaceae)

The Birch Family is characterized by thin, gracefu. light green foliage, clustered male flowers in pendent catkins, and conelike multiple fruits with winged seeds, or sometimes a nut surrounded by a leafy sheath. Birches have notably beautiful bark marked by horizontal lenticles. The smooth mottled bark of alders is familiar along streams. The hornbeams are small tolerant trees of the shaded forest understory. Hazels produce the edible filberts of commerce. The bark of the eastern Paper Birch was used by Indians for their graceful canoes.

European White Birch *(Betula verrucosa* or *B. pendula)*

This is a graceful tree with white trunk, pendulous branchlets, and numerous horticultural forms of foliage. The papery white bark is marked with horizontal lenticels and with black ridges here and there. It may reach a height of 40 feet or more, with a pyramidal open crown of shimmering leaves, but is usually smaller as seen in gardens and on street plantings.

Figure 22 European White Birch

Leaves and fruit: The simple, thin light green leaves are alternate in arrangement on the slender twigs, 2½ inches long including the petiole and 1½ inches wide. Leaf margins are doubly serrate, and some varieties are deeply cut almost to the midrib. Male and female flowers occur in drooping catkins on the same tree; the female ripens in autumn as woody brown conelets about an inch long. These persist on the tree after the leaves turn gold and fall, breaking up gradually during the winter to release winged seeds.

Other and quite similar birches occasionally met with are *B. papyrifera*, the White Birch, or Paper Birch, from eastern North America, with larger and coarser leaves; and *B. platyphylla*, the Japanese White Birch.

The timber birches, however, are not in cultivation. All are shade-enduring species which do not thrive under hot, dry conditions. Other small trees in the family are: *Carpinus betulus*, the European Hornbeam, with dark smooth bark and clustered, pendent flowers having leafy appendages; *C.caroliniana*, the American Hornbeam, or Blue Beech; and *Ostrya virginiana*, the Hop Hornbeam, with finely striated bark and fruits resembling those of the hop vine; *Corylus maxima*, the Giant Filbert, a small tree, usually much-branched, with doubly serrate hairy leaves or finely serrate leaf margins, and edible nuts borne in pairs included in leafy sheaths.

BEECH-OAK FAMILY (Fagaceae)
(See also p. 87)

The deciduous species in this large family far outnumber the evergreens and include some of the largest and most important hardwood timber trees of the world. Beeches, chestnuts , and oaks are northern hemisphere trees; the genus *Nothofagus* is native in South America and Australia. Flowers are mostly inconspicuous, with both sexes occurring on the same tree: the male pendent on a threadlike raceme or clustered on an erect spike; the female borne singly or two to three on a short stalk. The fruit is a one-seeded plump nut enclosed in a spiny bur, or an acorn set in a fringed or scaly cap. Many are fine ornamentals and reach great size and age when on good sites.

Spanish Chestnut *(Castanea sativa)*
This is a large and important tree from the Mediterranean which produces sweet, edible nuts. They are

Figure 23 Spanish Chestnut

an important item of food in the Mediterranean countries, and are occasionally produced for sale on the

Pacific Coast. The tree was extensively planted in California by settlers from southern Europe, and many fine old trees survive near ranch houses.

Leaves and fruit: The bright green leaves, alternate in arrangement on stout, smooth brownish twigs, are 6 to 8 inches long by 2 inches wide; the coarsely serrate margins have straight veins running from the prominent midrib to each tooth. They are tomentose on the lower side, tapering both to the tip and to the short, ½-inch petiole. Male flowers are borne in feathery clusters on erect spikes; female flowers, on short stalks at the base of the spike. These ripen the first autumn as spiny burs about 2 inches in diameter containing two or three plump dark brown seeds.

American Chestnut *(Castanea dentata)*

This is a large tree of similar characteristics to the preceding species, but with somewhat larger and glossier leaves and large sweet nuts. Formerly an important source of lumber and tanbark in the eastern United States, it has been virtually exterminated by the chestnut blight, *Endothia parasitica*. Occasional trees are seen in California parks and gardens, as the disease has not spread to this area. The disease attacks the Spanish Chestnut also, but is not quite so virulent on that species.

A program of hybridization has been under way for about twenty-five years using strains of the smaller *C. mollissima*, the Chinese Chestnut, which is less susceptible to the blight in an attempt to develop a good tree which will be resistant to the disease, but with little success thus far. The Chinese Chestnut, a smaller tree with shorter leaves, is occasionally seen here.

THE BEECHES *(Fagus)*

Beech trees are important for their smooth-grained

[107]

hard timber, which is an important resource in Europe, eastern North America, Turkey, and Japan. Some are attractive ornamentals. All need consistent summer irrigation to succeed in California.

European Beech (*Fagus sylvatica*)

This is the noble timber and ornamental tree of Europe with spreading form, smooth gray bark, and a number of landscape varieties. It may reach 75 to 100 feet in height, and the forms with copper-colored or purple foliage make notable specimens. American and Japanese beeches are quite similar, but are rarely seen in cultivation here. The smooth-barked, slender twigs bear long, lance-pointed buds.

Leaves and fruit: The simple, alternate leaves are glossy deep green or various shades of red to purple. Their wavy margins are finely hairy and sometimes remotely toothed. They are oval in shape, on slender stems, 3 to 4 inches long and half as wide, and usually persist on the tree through much of the winter. The fruit is a spiny bur about ¾ inch long which contains triangular-shaped, sweet edible nuts.

THE OAKS (*Quercus*)

The oaks are widely distributed throughout the northern hemisphere. Many of the 200 or more species reach massive size, notable beauty, and great longevity. Many species provide hardwood lumber of outstanding quality, others are fine ornamentals, and some are reduced to the size of shrubs, particularly on poor soils and dry sites.

The White Oaks usually have light gray scaly or furrowed trunk bark, lobed leaves without spiny tips on the lobes, and acorns ripening the first autumn. The shell is smooth within, and the nut is not notably bitter. Included is a group of Chestnut Oaks in which the leaves resemble those of chestnut. The lumber shows broad medullary rays on radial section.

The Black or Red Oaks usually have hard, dark-colored bark which is smooth on young branches and eventually furrowed but not scaly. The lobes of the leaves are tipped with a slender spiny point. The acorns ripen the second autumn; their inner shells are coated with fine wooly hairs, and the nut has a bitter taste. In a subgroup known as Willow Oaks the leaves are narrow and willow-like. Only three species in each group are commonly cultivated here.

English Oak *(Quercus robur)*

This tree from Europe is famed in song and story for its great size and stately beauty. It furnished the lumber for the beautiful carvings and finish seen in old cathedrals and castles. It thrives here and grows to a fine tree with spreading crown, sturdy trunk, and branches enclosed by furrowed dark gray bark. There

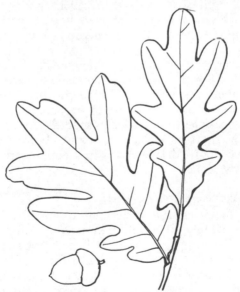

Figure 24 English Oak

are a number of horticultural forms, varying in habit of growth and shape of crown.

Leaves and fruit: The short-stalked leaves are glossy dark green above and bluish-green beneath, 3 to 5 inches long and half as wide, broader above the middle, and with three to seven shallow, rounded lobes on each side. The petiole, about ¼ inch or less in length, often appears to be set in a basal notch. The inconspicuous flowers may be in clusters of two to five on a slender stalk, or single and sessile: the male clustered on wispy pendent threads in spring; the female ripening the first autumn as acorns about an inch long, one-third enclosed in the cup.

Turkey Oak (*Quercus cerris*)

This tree from southern Europe and western Asia is a fine round-headed hardy oak which reaches 100 feet in height and produces excellent lumber in its native habitat. It is well adapted here, especially in hot interior valleys with summer irrigation on good soils.

Leaves and fruit: The oblong-oval dark green leaves, 4 to 5 inches long and half as wide, are almost smooth above and coated with fine gray hairs beneath; their margins have three to eight pairs of shallow lobes, sometimes with widely spaced teeth on the lobes. The short-stalked acorns, about 1½ inches long, are borne singly, half-enclosed in a cup covered with fine mossy scales.

Bur Oak (*Quercus macrocarpa*)

This tree from the eastern and southern United States is widely distributed from New England to eastern Wyoming and Texas. It becomes a large tree on good soils, but persists in smaller form under more difficult situations. The dark brown bark is deeply furrowed, and most trees show corky wings on the twigs. It grows well on a variety of sites in this region, with sturdy form.

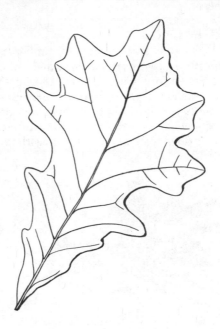

Figure 25 Bur Oak

Leaves and fruit: The leaves are 6 to 10 inches long, bright green and glossy above, gray or white and finely haired beneath, somewhat kite-shaped in outline, usually with a deep middle sinus cutting almost to the midrib. The short-stalked acorn, maturing the first autumn, is 1 to 1½ inches long, enclosed for about half its length in a large cup coated with fringed, mossy scales.

White Oak *(Quercus alba)*
This is the fine timber species of eastern America,

[111]

with furrowed gray bark and fine symmetrically lobed leaves and small sweet acorns. It is only occasionally seen here.

Northern Red Oak *(Quercus rubra or Q. borealis)*
This is a tall, smooth-barked timber species from the forests of the northeastern and middle western United States and Canada. It has fine upright form with smooth dark green bark on the upper branches, and reaches a height of 70 or more feet on good sites. An excellent street tree, with quite rapid growth for an oak, it does well in this region with some summer irrigation.

Figure 26 Northern Red Oak

Leaves and fruit: The shiny dark green leaves are 7 to 9 inches long and half as wide, glossy below and above when fully grown; the spiny-tipped lobes are separated by rounded sinuses extending about halfway to the midrib. Short-stalked plump acorns about an inch long are set in a shallow saucer-shaped cup.

Scarlet Oak *(Quercus coccinea)*
This tree from, the eastern United States, is a favorite street and ornamental tree because of its moder-

ate size, controlled growth, and the fine color effects of its autumn foliage. The delicate tracery of branches forms a spreading open crown. The bark is smooth and dark. The tree may reach a height of 50 feet or more, but is slow-growing and easily controlled to required size by pruning. It does well in interior valleys with summer irrigation.

Leaves and fruit: The 3- to 6-inch smooth light green leaves are 2 to 4 inches wide, borne on slender petioles and deeply cut by rounded sinuses separating the seven to nine spiny-tipped and tapered lobes. The plump, rounded acorns are borne on short stalks, ¾ inch long, about one-third enclosed in an almost smooth cup.

Pin Oak *(Quercus palustris)*

Also from the middle-western United States, this tree is similar in conformation and leaf type to the preceding species. Its graceful symmetry of crown has made it one of the favorite trees for street and highway planting. The common name comes from the short, stiff branchlets which extend horizontally from the trunk, among the other branches, like a series of pins. The branches are slender, the lower ones somewhat pendulous, and the deeply cut leaves give an open, shimmering effect to the symmetrical crown. The gray-brown bark is shallowly ridged on the trunk but smooth above. The tree is hardy, but needs summer irrigation here as do most other oaks.

Leaves and fruit: The leaves are about 5 inches long including the short, slender petiole, shiny green above and paler green beneath, with tufts of fine hairs in the axils of the veins. The spiny-tipped lobes appear to be more at right angles to the midrib than in the preceding species, and the crown is less dense. The foliage turns deep red or bronze in autumn. The short-stalked globular acorns, ⅓ to ½ inch long, are about one-third enclosed in a saucer-shaped cup. They mature the second fall.

ELM FAMILY (Ulmaceae)

Trees in this family, which includes the elms, hackberries, and Zelkova are characterized by simple alternate leaves, short-stalked, broad-bladed, and serrate, usually asymmetrical at the base. Inconspicuous clustered flowers develop into symmetrically winged nutlets or small hard berries. Many are tall, handsome trees with spreading crowns, but they are being decimated by attacks of the Dutch elm disease and the elm-leaf beetle. We are fortunate that the Dutch elm disease has not yet reached California, but the beetle requires control by spraying.

American Elm *(Ulmus americana)*

From central and northeastern America, this is a large and stately tree with dark, furrowed bark and vase-shaped, spreading crown of great beauty. In the central hardwood forest, elms were often 100 feet tall and produced hardwood lumber with figured grain of excellent quality. Now it is disappearing because of insect and disease attacks, but many fine trees are still in good condition in this region. Formerly extensively planted as a street tree, the large size has caused their removal from many congested districts.

Leaves and fruit: The simple bright green leaves are borne in alternate arrangement on slender twigs. They are 3 to 5 inches long and half as wide, with expanded blades on short petioles and doubly serrate margins. They are unequal at the base, smooth or slightly roughened above, pubescent or nearly smooth beneath, and lacking tufts of hairs in the axils of the veins. Fruits are flat and leaflike, up to ½ inch long, with fine hairs on the margins. They ripen in early spring before the leaves unfold. Root suckers are produced at the base.

Figure 27 American Elm

English Elm (*Ulmus procera* or *U. campestris*)

This tree from Europe is similar to the preceding species. It has deeply furrowed bark and a massive oval crown, and may reach a height of over 100 feet. It is about as common in this area as the American Elm along streets and in parks.

Leaves and fruit: The leaves are similar to those of the preceding species, with asymmetrical base, short petiole, and doubly serrate margins. They are rougher above and have tufts of hairs in the leaf axils beneath. The twigs are sometimes corky. The flat leaflike fruits are larger, up to 1 inch long, without hairs on the margins. They ripen in quantities in early spring.

Scotch or Wych Elm *(Ulmus glabra)*

This tree from Europe resembles the two preceding species. The broadly oval, sharp-pointed leaves have doubly serrate margins, and the fruits are smooth and leafy. The tree has a number of ornamental forms, of which the round-headed, weeping (cult. var.) "Camperdownii' is most frequently seen as a park and garden specimen of interesting dwarf form.

Chinese Elm *(Ulmus parvifolia)*

From Asia, this is a variable tree with several ornamental forms having small shiny leaves which are evergreen near the coast and in mild areas, but deciduous elsewhere. It grows rapidly, withstanding heat and some drought, and may grow to a height of 50 feet or more. The crown is glossy, and the trunk smooth, with mottled green and tan bark. A popular garden form is a small tree with flat, umbrella-like crown. It has the smallest leaves of any of the elms.

Leaves and fruit: The leathery leaves, usually 2 inches or less in length, are singly serrate on the margins and but slightly asymmetrical at the base. They are glossy above and paler beneath, and taper both to the short petiole and the blunt tip. The flowers occur after the leaves, and the fruit ripens in the fall; in frosty inland sections it turns red and persists on the tree as an attractive feature after the leaves fall.

Siberian Elm *(Ulmus pumila)*

This tree from Asia is a fast-growing and hardy elm which is now planted extensively throughout the middle west, the Great Basin area, and the southwest, as well as in California for its ability to withstand heat and drought with some irrigation. It may reach a height of 50 feet or more, but there are small shrubby types as well. It has a wide-spreading root system and develops a broad crown of brittle branches which are apt to break in winds, but it makes a fairly good tree in areas where few other trees will grow. The bark is rough and furrowed.

Leaves and fruit: The leaves are firm when fully grown, about 3 inches long by 1 inch or less in width, dark green and smooth above and paler beneath. They taper both to the short petiole and the blunt tip, and are usually singly serrate. The flat, leafy fruit, with a deep open notch at the tip, ripens in midsummer among the leaves.

Ulmus thomasi, the Rock Elm, and *U. crassifolia*, the Cedar Elm, both with corky wings on the twigs, are occasionally seen here.

The hackberries are distinguished by thin elmlike leaves which may be entire or singly serrate, virtually symmetrical at the base with gray-green color, thin gray bark which is smooth or marked with warty protuberances, inconspicuous flowers, and small berry-like drupe fruits which are borne singly on slender stems in the axils of the leaves. Very few of the more than sixty species are in cultivation here.

European Hackberry *(Celtis australis)*

This tree from southern Europe has elmlike foliage, smooth gray bark marked by occasional warty protuberances, a rounded crown of small horizontal branches, and dense foliage. The dense crown casts heavy shade which is welcome in valley areas. It is a hardy and dependable drought-resistant tree, requires little maintenance, makes a good street tree of moderate rate of growth, and on good soil may reach a height of 75 feet.

Leaves and fruit: The simple, alternate leaves, up to 6 inches long, have short, slender petioles, are

[117]

wedge-shaped toward the base, and taper above the middle to a slender point. Margins are entire toward

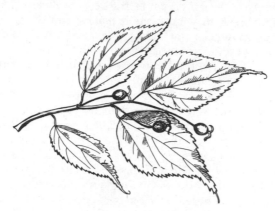

Figure 28 European Hackberry

the base, but singly and sharply serrate above this. The leaves are gray-green, with soft pubescence beneath. The fruit is a purplish berry ½ inch in diameter with a single seed, borne on a slender stem in the axils of the leaves.

Other hackberries are similar, with the following major distinctions: *C. sinensis*, the Chinese Hackberry, has leaves with toothed and wavy margins, fine pubescence beneath, and orange-colored fruits; *C. occidentalis*, the American Hackberry, is a large tree to 100 feet or more, and has leaves to 5 inches long, glossy green above, paler beneath, and orange-red to deep purple fruits; and *C. laevigata*, the Sugarberry, has leaves usually entire and slender-pointed, thin, 4 inches long, and orange-red sugary fruits.

Sawleaf Zelkova or **Japanese Zelkova** *(Zelkova serrata)*
This is one of three or four elmlike trees from Asia, and is the only one commonly seen here. It grows easily in many areas and becomes a handsome tree,

up to 75 feet tall, with a spreading crown of dense foliage which turns an attractive bronze or red color in fall. Bark on the stout trunk is dark brown and scaly. This hardy and pest-free species stands heat, drought, and poor soils, including those with some alkali. It makes a good street or windbreak tree, and may be pruned to a hedge.

Leaves and fruit: The leaves are simple, alternate in arrangement on slender, smooth branchlets and slender petioles. On flowering branches they are 2 to 3 inches long and half as wide, but in the main crown they are 6 inches long by 3 inches wide. They are dark green and roughened above, lighter green and smooth beneath, with three prominent veins. The margins are coarsely toothed with each tooth ending in a sharp point. The petioles are short and twisted so that the leaves are arranged in two-ranked flat sprays. Small inconspicuous greenish flowers in the leaf axils ripen as stalked oblique drupes about ⅛ inch in diameter.

MULBERRY FAMILY (Moraceae)

This large, mostly tropical family includes a number of trees with edible fruits — banyan, breadfruit, and fig, as well as the mulberries. The deciduous members have large, long-stalked, often lobed leaves, milky sap, and small multiple flowers which ripen as berry-like or figlike fruits with many small seeds.

White Mulberry (*Morus alba*)

This tree from China is attractive, round-headed or spreading, with dense crown and light tan bark, which grows to a height of 50 feet or more. A hardy tree with good adaptability, it has few enemies. The foliage is the food of the silkworm and the tree was formerly planted in California in attempts to cultivate that insect. The berries attract birds.

Leaves and fruit: The glossy bright green leaves

[119]

are 2½ to 6 inches long with petioles ½ to 1 inch long, ovate in shape with a flattened base, some irregularly lobed (mitten-like)or entire and with finely toothed margins, often with pubescent veins beneath. The succulent white fruits become pinkish or purplish when ripe, and are sweet to the taste.

There are several varieties: *pendula,* an ornamental with weeping branches; (cult. var.) "Tatarica," Russian Mulberry, a very hardy form with smaller leaves and bushy habit of growth; and two rather recent clones (cult. var.) "Kingan" and "Stribling," with large shining, variously lobed or entire leaves which grow rapidly and do not bear fruit. They are now being used extensively in subdivision planting, and with good care make nice ornamentals with dense, glossy dark green foliage.

Black Mulberry *(Morus nigra)*

This tree from Asia has leaves which are somewhat rough above and pubescent beneath, 3 to 6 inches long and half as wide, with heart-shaped bases. Leaves are entire with toothed margins, or occasionally lobed. The 1-inch berries are dark red to almost black.

Morus rubra, the Red Mulberry, from the eastern United States, has similar characteristics, but the leaves are oval or with flat bases and not heart-shaped, and are sharply serrate on the margins, sometimes variously lobed, and coated with soft pubescence beneath. The 1-inch fruits are red or reddish purple.

Paper Mulberry *(Broussonetia papyrifera)*

From China and Japan, this is a hardy tree up to 50 feet tall. The bark is used in its native Asia for making paper. The tree has a milky juice, grows easily from seed, and is naturalized in many areas of the United States. There are several horticultural varieties.

Leaves and fruit: The large oval or irregularly

lobed light green leaves are coated above and beneath with feltlike pubescence and have toothed margins. The multiple tomentose fruits consist of small orange-red drupelets.

Common Fig *(Ficus carica)*

This tree from western Asia is low and spreading with smooth gray branches. It produces the edible figs of commerce. It is commonly planted as a garden ornamental for its deeply-lobed leaves, multiple stems with smooth bark, and succulent fruits. In orchards the figs are kept pruned to about 10 feet, with spreading crowns, but when allowed to grow naturally the tree will reach a height of 30 to 40 feet and about the same crown diameter. There are a number of named varieties.

Leaves and fruit: The long-stalked leaves, a deep rich green in color, may be 12 inches long and almost the same width. They are alternate in arrangement, have very deep sinuses between the spreading lobes, are roughened above and hairy beneath, with wavy or finely toothed margins and heart-shaped base. The purple or white fruit is a fleshy edible receptacle, rather pear-shaped, containing many small seeds. It is 1½ to 3 inches long.

Osage Orange *(Maclura pomifera)*

This is an interesting and very hardy tree from the south-central United States, where it is an extensive use as a windbreak tree, often known as "Hedge." Hedgerows of this tree are common in rural sections. On good soils it grows to a height of 50 or more feet. When trees are closely spaced their dense crowns of stout interlacing branches make a very effective barrier. Trunk bark is orange-brown and lightly furrowed, and the smooth, light green to tan branchlets are armed with prickly spines. The yellow bark of the extensive root system was used by the Indians as a source of yellow dye. The dense greenish-tan heartwood is strong and elastic and was formerly much used in the making of archery bows; it is so durable that it makes one of the best fence posts.

Leaves and fruit: The alternate light green leaves are 4 to 5 inches long and half as wide, on slender petioles ¾ to 2 inches long with entire margins and tapered both to the stem and rather blunt tip. They are glossy above and often slightly pubescent beneath, and turn yellow before dropping in autumn. Inconspicuous flowers occur on separate trees. Male flowers are in pendent racemes up to 1½ inches long; the female in globular heads, become hard, fibrous, orange-like green fruits up to 4 inches in diameter, with a rough, warty exterior, and contain many seeds. They are inedible and orange-tan in color when mature.

MAGNOLIA FAMILY (Magnoliaceae)
(See also p. 76)

The deciduous members of this family have large, entire or lobed leaves, often showy tulip-like flowers with flower parts in threes or sixes. Some are tall timber trees with wood of excellent quality. Others are small but beautiful flowering ornamentals.

Tulip Tree or **Yellow Poplar** *(Liriodendron tulipifera)*

This is one of the finest hardwood timber trees of the eastern United States. On good deep soil of "coves" in that area it becomes a stately tree, 150 feet or more in height and of large diameter, from which fine Yellow Poplar or "whitewood" cabinet lumber is obtained. The conical or spreading crown turns an attractive yellow color in fall. The gray-brown bark is smooth on the branches and divided by shallow furrows into diamond-shaped figures on the trunk. The smooth twigs terminate in flat buds shaped like a duck's bill. In central California it makes an attractive specimen in parks and large gardens and is occasionally planted as a street tree. It does best on soil of good quality with adequate summer moisture, but tolerates heat and cold and has few enemies.

Leaves and fruit: The bright green leaves are 8 inches long including the slender petiole which clasps the stem at its base. The broad blade is rounded at the base with four lobes and a distinctive recessed tip. They are alternate in arrangement and have entire margins. Tulip-shaped greenish-yellow flowers, about 2 inches wide, marked with orange at the base, occur singly among the leaves in summer. They ripen as erect, multiple fruits with brown-winged seeds which fall gradually in winter.

The attractive shrubby deciduous magnolias from China and Japan, notably *Magnolia soulangeana*, the hybrid Saucer Magnolia, have large, erect, showy pink or lavender blooms appearing before the leaves in spring, and are sometimes referred to as tulip trees.

WITCH HAZEL FAMILY (Hamamelidaceae)

This family of trees and shrubs includes some twenty genera found in warm temperate regions. Leaves are alternate, and flowers and seeds are in ball-like multiple heads; some seeds are winged. *Hamamelis virginiana*, the Witch Hazel shrub of the eastern hardwood forest area, expels its seeds from the capsule when ripe. The leaves and bark have medicinal qualities, and Sweet Gum trees are the source of a fragrant balsam (storax).

Sweet Gum *(Liquidambar styraciflua)*

This is a tall straight timber tree with wide distribution on lowlands and river-bottom swamps from central New England to southern Texas, where large trees supply the "gum" lumber with attractive figured grain used as an interior finish. Although a large tree in its native habitat, it grows rather slowly in this region to heights of 40 feet or more. The twigs usually show corky wings, which, with the pendent ball-like fruit clusters will identify the tree when leafless. The bark is deeply furrowed. This tree is extensively planted along streets and in gardens for the beauty of its star-shaped leaves and their brilliant fall coloration.

Figure 29 Sweet Gum

Leaves and fruit: The simple, alternate dark green leaves are star-shaped, 4 to 6 inches long and about as wide, on long slender stems. The blades are "maple-like," divided into five pointed lobes with finely toothed margins. Even in mild climates they turn in fall to brilliant colors of scarlet, pink, orange, yellow, and red. Tiny yellow flowers are borne in spring in globular heads and ripen as spiny balls about an inch in diameter on pendent stalks. These hang on the trees in winter, and the beaked capsules gradually open to release the winged seeds.

Two other species, *L. orientalis*, from Turkey, and *L. formosana*, from Formosa, are being used in the development of new hybrid varieties, and clones with

[124]

especially fine autumn coloration are being grown by selection and vegetative propagation at Saratoga.

ROSE FAMILY (Rosaceae)
(See also p. 82)

The deciduous species of this large family include many important fruit and ornamental trees and shrubs. The leaves are alternate, simple or compound, the flower parts usually in fives, with white, pink, or red petals, often flowering before the leaves. The familiar fruit trees—apple, pear, cherry, peach, plum, apricot, almond, and quince—are frequently used as ornamentals and some as street trees, but will not be treated in this volume. The genus *Prunus* includes many flowering cherries from Japan, the flowering peach, and the flowering almond—all with brilliant floral displays in spring, and some with purple foliage which are favorite small street trees.

The large and complex genus *Crataegus* includes shrubs and small thorny-stemmed trees known as thorn apples which are widely distributed in the northern hemisphere. There are a number of horticultural varieties and probably hybrid forms. Thorn apples have simple, lobed bright green leaves with toothed or serrate margins, greenish-yellow bark on the smaller branches, and globular fruits resembling little apples which are red, orange, or yellow when ripe and contain numerous seeds.

English Hawthorne *(Crataegus oxycantha)*

This tree from Europe forms a dense rounded crown up to 25 feet with upright thorny branches and smooth brownish twigs which display clusters of flowers in spring.

Leaves and fruit: The thin light green leaves are three- to five-lobed on slender petioles, 1 to 2 inches long and about half as wide, with finely toothed

[125]

margins. The flowers are white or red, either single or double. Small scarlet berries are borne on slender stems in dense clusters. They are about ½ inch long, but variable in different varieties of the tree.

Washington Thorn (*Crataegus phaenopyrum*)

This handsome tree from the eastern United States has a straight trunk and dense, nicely rounded crown of horizontal branches and shiny foliage. It may reach 20 to 30 feet in height, with a spread of 20 feet, and has ornamental flowers and fruits. It is not injured by frost, but does best back from the coast, where it tolerates heat and drought and even some alkali in the soil. It is wind firm, but does not reach its best development near the seacoast.

Leaves and fruit: The thin light green three- to five-lobed leaves are alternate in arrangement, 1 to 2½ inches long and an equal width, with long petioles and serrate margins. They turn red or orange in autumn. Flowers bloom in large clusters all over the tree in May and June after the leaves are fully grown. Bright red berries ¼ inch in diameter are borne in dense, drooping clusters on long stems, making a very attractive color display well into the winter months.

Lavalle or Carriere Thorn (*Crataegus* x *lavallei*)

This is a hybrid of beautiful conformation which is hardy throughout this area, but produces better flowers and fruits in the cooler sections. It grows to a height of 25 to 30 feet, and needs occasional pruning to prevent too great density. The brownish bark is smooth on young trees and branches, but becomes somewhat scaly on larger specimens. The slender crown of criss-cross branches becomes red in the fall.

Leaves and fruit: The simple alternate leaves are entire, with wedge-shaped bases and serrate margins tapering to a blunt tip. They are 2 to 4 inches long

[126]

and half as wide. Grayish-green in summer, they become bronze-red in fall and persist for some time. The clustered white flowers with red centers make a fine display in May. They ripen as orange-red berries nearly 1 inch long, borne in great profusion and persisting through the winter, so they are often cut for Christmas decorations.

Flowering Crabapples *(Malus* sp.)

These crabapples from Asia, Europe and America include some ten species of small trees which resemble the hawthorns, and a number of hybrid forms. They may grow to 20 feet, with fine floral displays. The red, orange, or yellow fruits give attractive fall color and some may be used in making jellies. There are many horticultural varieties and they comprise some of the most popular ornamental garden trees. There are types with rounded or columnar crowns, and others with weeping branches.

Leaves and fruit: The simple, alternate leaves, oval in shape, with long slender petioles, have finely toothed margins. They are 2 to 4 inches long, and about half as wide at the middle of the blade. The color varies from light through dark green to red or purple in some varieties. The clustered flowers on slender stems may be white, pink, or deep red. The fruits are little apples on long slender stems with variable color tones.

European Mountain Ash or Rowan Tree *(Sorbus aucuparia)*

From Europe and Asia, this is a small round-headed tree up to 30 or more feet in height, with finely divided open foliage. The smooth gray-brown bark is marked with lenticels. It is called "Ash" because of the compound leaves. This fine ornamental tree has a number of horticultural forms which are quite hardy, but it does best in areas back from the coast. Occasional specimens of the Western Mountain Ash (S. *sitchensis*) may be seen.

Leaves and fruit: The alternate, pinnate compound leaves, up to 7 inches long, consist of nine to fifteen pointed gray-green leaflets which are opposite in arrangement on the slender rachis. The foliage turns bright orange or red in autumn. Tiny white flowers appear in dense, flat-topped clusters in spring, and ripen as flat clusters of bright red berries ½ inch in diameter.

BEAN OR PEA FAMILY (Leguminosae)
(See also p. 65)

The deciduous trees in this large family usually have pealike flowers, usually compound leaves in alternate arrangement, and hard seeds which ripen in a dry or fleshy pod. The roots of some species have tubercles with nitrogen-fixing bacteria.

Black or Yellow Locust (*Robinia pseudoacacia*)

This tree from the middle western United States is a hardy species, probably brought to California by the early pioneers, as it is one of the most common trees in many valley and foothill towns, where there are many fine old specimens. It grows easily from seed and develops into a tree 50 or more feet in height with furrowed brownish bark on the trunk, a much-branched, rounded light green crown with smooth twigs usually armed with sharp thorns borne in pairs at the base of each leaf. Some varieties are thornless. Young growth is rapid on good soil, but the tree persists in spite of poor soil, heat, drought, and some alkali. Root sprouts are common. The greenish heartwood is very hard and strong and makes a long-lived fence post. Several horticultural varieties are available, including (cult. var.) "Decaisneana," with fragrant pink flowers, and (cult. var.) "Inermis," in which the thorns are lacking.

Leaves and fruit: The compound alternate light green leaves, 5 to 12 inches long, consist of seven to nine thin oval leaflets with entire margins. The fragrant pealike flowers, white or pink, occur in drooping clusters in spring, and ripen as flat 4-inch brown pods containing several hard black seeds. The pods persist on the tree long after the leaves fall.

Hairy Locust *(Robinia neomexicana)*

This is a similar but smaller tree with pubescent leaves and twigs, stipular spines at the leaf base, and rose-pink flowers which ripen as 4-inch pods with hairy pubescence.

Robinia hispida var *macrophylla,* a small grafted specimen with sweeping branchlets and masses of rose-colored flowers, is known as Rose Acacia.

Honey Locust *(Gleditsia triacanthos)*

This handsome tree from the middle western United States, 60 feet or more in height, has an open crown of wide-spreading branches with fernlike feathery foliage. The dark trunk is furrowed into long smooth scaly ridges. The formation of the multiple trunks may be prevented by pruning. The specific name comes from the heavy, sharp, three-branched thorns with which the trunk and lower branches are often armed. These form a well-nigh impenetrable barrier when trees are closely spaced, but the thornless (cult. var.) "Inermis" is now usually preferred. There are several other horticultural varieties, of which the (cult. var.) "Moraine" clone is probably the most popular, because of its rapid growth and attractive form as a street tree. It too is thornless. The tree is hardy and has few enemies.

Leaves and fruit: The feather-compound leaves

are up to 10 inches long, with twenty-one or more thin taper-pointed leaflets about an inch long and ¼ to ½ inch wide; the entire margins are arranged oppositely along a slender rachis. The leaves turn from light green to yellow in the fall. Clusters of small greenish flowers are borne in racemes, and are attractive to bees for their fragrant nectar. These ripen into twisted dark brown seed pods, 12 to 16 inches long by 1½ inches wide, with large, hard oval seeds embedded in a rather sweet pulp. The long shiny pods hang on the tree after the leaves have fallen.

Mimosa or Silk Tree *(Albizia julibrissin)*

Native from Iran to Japan, this is a wide-spreading tree sometimes 40 feet tall but usually shorter, with rounded crown of foliage and tan-colored bark. It is fast-growing but not long-lived; with care it will survive poor soil, heat, drought, and considerable frost.

Leaves and fruit: The feathery, twice-compound leaves, bright green in color, are alternate in arrangement, each leaflet quite small, with the midrib close to one edge. The leaf stem has a small gland near its base. Tiny pink flowers are borne in dense fluffy heads resembling pin cushions, an inch or more wide, which are crowded on the upper branches. Fruits are flat brown pods, 5 to 6 inches long, containing hard oval seeds.

Golden Chain or Bean Tree *(Laburnum anagyroides)*

This is a scraggly and much-branched tree from southern Europe which may grow up to 30 feet tall, with pendent sprays of fragrant golden flowers in spring, smooth greenish twigs, and olive-green bark. It is hardy, must be pruned to shape at intervals, and requires good summer irrigation. It is most commonly seen as a small garden tree.

Leaves and fruit: The trifoliate compound leaves

are made up of three oval, short-stalked entire leaflets borne at the end of a long slender petiole. The leaflets are light green above, gray-green and pubescent beneath. The pealike light yellow flowers, an inch across, are borne in weeping, chainlike sprays in early summer. They ripen as twisted brown pods 2 inches long by ½ inch wide, with small hard black seeds. Pods persist after the leaves fall.

A similar hybrid, *L.* x *watereri*, which has longer chains of flowers, is known as the Longcluster Golden Chain Tree.

Japanese Pagoda Tree or Chinese Scholar Tree *(Sophora japonica)*

This tree from the Orient is similar to the Black Locust in appearance, growth characteristics, and hardiness. Slower-growing than the locust, it eventually reaches a height of 50 feet or more. It is an attractive tree with a rounded crown, shiny dark green twigs which lack thorns, and dark, furrowed bark.

Leaves and fruit: The compound leaves, although similar to those of the Black Locust, are darker green and the 2-inch leaflets taper to a pointed tip; they are glossy above and hairy beneath. Loose clusters of light yellow flowers ¼ inch across occur in late summer in erect spikes 10 to 12 inches long. The fruits are plump, cylindrical 3-inch pods which are constricted between the plump seeds and are soapy when crushed. They persist through the winter.

Other deciduous trees of the Bean Family which are occasionally seen in cultivation here include *Cercis canadensis*, the Eastern Redbud, from the eastern United States; *C. chinensis*, the Chinese Redbud, from China; and *C. siliquastrum*, the Judas Tree, from the Mediterranean. All are small trees similar to the native redbud of the foothills, with rounded leaves, purple-red (rarely white) flowers in spring before the leaves, and persistent flat brown pods containing hard oval seeds.

Yellow Wood *(Cladrastis lutea)*
This tree from the southeastern United States has compound leaves made up of seven broadly ovate leaflets in alternate arrangement on the rachis, 8 to 12 inches long. The fragrant white flowers, 1¼ inch long, in drooping panicles 12 to 18 inches long, ripen as narrow flat pods 2 to 4 inches long, containing hard seeds.

Orchid Tree *(Bauhinia purpurea)*
This tree from India and China, the hardiest of the Bauhinias, has simple heart-shaped leaves, notched at the tip; white, red, or purple flowers in fragrant clusters; and flat pods 4 to 10 inches long. It does best in very sheltered situations.

Jerusalem Thorn or **Horse Bean** *(Parkinsonia aculeata)*
This tree of the southwestern deserts, has spreading green-barked stems, long needle-like compound leaves with many tiny leaflets, 6 to 12 inches long and quickly deciduous; masses of yellow flowers in slender erect racemes 3 to 6 inches long; and slender, plump pods which are constricted between seeds.

QUASSIA FAMILY (Simarubaceae)
The Quassia Family includes about thirty genera of trees and shrubs, mainly tropical, usually with compound, alternate leaves, small clustered flowers, and winged or drupelike fruits. Many have a bitter principle in the bark or wood, and are sometimes useful in insecticides, medicines, and dyes.

Tree of Heaven *(Ailanthus altissima)*
This tree from northern China has been extensively

planted around the world for its hardiness. One of the few trees which thrive surrounded by the smoke and pavements of cities, it persists in spite of poor soil, heat, drought, cold, and abuse, spreading by root suckers or seeds to take over vacant property, so it has become one of the best-known trees of temperate areas throughout the world. It grows to a height of 40 feet or more, often occurring in dense clumps, and may be recognized by its very long compound foliage, stout twigs with smooth or warty bark, and attractive clusters of leafy red fruits which appear on female trees only. It has few enemies and is difficult to eradicate if male and female trees are growing in the same location.

Leaves and fruit: The compound alternate leaves, up to 36 inches long, consist of from eleven to thirty-one bright green leaflets, 3 to 5 inches long and half as wide, which are rounded at the base and tapered to the tip, with entire margins except for a gland near the base. The small yellowish flowers are borne in dense terminal panicles, with male and female on separate trees. The male flowers have an unpleasant odor when crushed. The fruits are decorative clusters of papery-winged, single-seeded reddish samaras twisted like the blades of an airplane propeller. They fall gradually from the trees during the winter.

MAHOGANY FAMILY (Meliaceae)

The most famous tree of this generally tropical family supplies the valuable lumber for furniture and cabinet work, although Spanish Cedar is also a fine hardwood with a fragrant odor. Only one of about forty genera is commonly cultivated here.

Texas Umbrella (*Melia azedarach* "Umbraculifera")

This tree is said to have originated in Texas as a clone of the Chinaberry or Bead Tree of the Himalayas and China. It is much more commonly planted than the species, particularly in valley areas, for the shade provided by its dense umbrella-like crown of rather pendent foliage. It is of moderate size, while the species is a tall tree with spreading crown and sturdy trunk. Both are hardy and survive on poor soil with minimum attention, but are short-lived. Large trees of the species are seen occasionally in old gardens.

Leaves and fruit: The shiny green leaves are alternate in arrangement, twice-compound, 20 to 36 inches long, composed of many sharply pointed leaflets with toothed margins. These are about 2 inches long and half as wide, sessile or short-stalked, with rounded bases. Small, fragrant lilac-colored flowers appear in loose clusters 4 to 8 inches long in late spring, and ripen as cream-colored beadlike berries ½ inch across which hang in clusters after the leaves fall.

Maple Family (Aceraceae)

Maples are distinguished by their opposite, usually broadly lobed, leaves on long slender petioles (those of *Acer negundo* are compound) and by the winged samara fruits which are borne in pairs, often in drooping clusters. More than a hundred maples are distributed throughout temperate regions of the northern hemisphere, and include several very important timber trees and many beautiful ornamentals. About fifty species of maple are cultivated as ornamentals in the United States. A very large collection is being grown at the University of Washington Arboretum in Seattle. Many maples are notable for the brilliant coloration of their autumn foliage, but they are less colorful in our mild California climate. Some species have landscape varieties showing incised or colored foliage or an interesting growth habit.

[134]

Silver Maple *(Acer saccharinum)*

This fast-growing tree from eastern North America has smooth gray bark on the branches and a wide-spreading crown. It may reach a height of 75 feet or more, with an equal spread of branches. Although it is very hardy, the wood is brittle, and branches are apt to break in high winds unless they are controlled by pruning. The tree has a wide-spreading root system and is not long-lived; so it should be planted with caution in spite of its beauty.

Leaves and fruit: The large, deeply lobed light green leaves are silvery below, with double-toothed margins and a sharp "gunsight" notch at the base of each sinus. Clustered yellow-green flowers in early spring ripen as double samaras, with an angle of about 45° between them, which persist on the trees into winter. In frosty locations the foliage turns brilliant shades of red, pink, and gold.

Figure 30 Silver Maple

Red or **Swamp Maple** *(Acer rubrum)*

This tree is typical of bottomlands and swamps

[135]

throughout eastern North America, where it is noted for the beauty of its fall foliage. It grows well here but needs consistent summer irrigation. Although naturally a large tree when mature, it is usually smaller in this region: 40 feet or less.

Leaves and fruit: The leaves are smaller and usually more shallowly lobed than in the preceding species, with doubly serrate margins and a sharp notch at the sinus base. They are reddish when they unfold, become bright green above and gray beneath, and some turn a handsome deep red in fall even without frost. Interesting clusters of tiny deep red flowers appear on the twigs in spring before the leaves. The paired fruits spread at about right angles from the slender stem. They are red in summer, turn brown in autumn, and persist after the leaves fall.

Japanese Maple *(Acer palmatum)*

This tree from Japan may reach a height of 25 feet. There are many landscape varieties, all of small size and fragile appearance. It is probably more com-

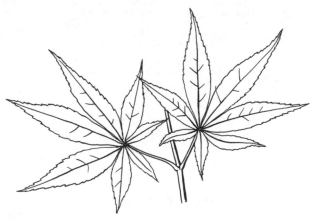

Figure 31 Japanese Maple

monly planted in this region than any other maple. Hardy as a street tree, it has even more appeal as a garden specimen because of its dainty and colorful foliage.

Leaves and fruit: The small, thin leaves are 5- to 7-lobed, with toothed margins and deeply cut sinuses, in some varieties reaching almost to the mid-rib. Leaves may be bright green, dark red, or purple. They are 2 to 4 inches long and so thin that many trees have a gauzy appearance. The small paired samara fruits are in clusters, spreading at a wide angle from the end of slender stalks.

Norway Maple *(Acer platanoides)*

This is a round-headed tree from Europe, up to 50 feet tall or more, with a dense crown of foliage. The smooth dark green twigs terminate in plump light green buds, and the sap is milky. It is a hardy tree with a rapid growth rate on soils of variable quality, but it needs water in summer. In the foothill towns it is an excellent street tree. There are a number of named varieties.

Leaves and fruit: The shiny, bright green leaves, opposite in arrangement on slender petioles, are 4 to 7 inches long, broadly five- to seven-lobed, with coarse marginal teeth and rounded sinuses. Some of the landscape varieties have reddish or purplish leaves; some are variegated, with white patches. In autumn the foliage turns bright yellow. Small greenish flowers occur in erect clusters before the leaves in spring, and ripen as double samaras in clusters on slender stalks with a spread of 160° between the two wings.

Sugar Maple *(Acer saccharum)*

This tree from North America is the source of fine hard maple lumber and also maple sugar and syrup from the sap in spring. Here it grows slowly to moder-

Figure 32 Norway Maple

ate size with a fine tracery of opposite branches, and makes a very good street tree.

Leaves and fruit: The leaves are smaller but similar to those of the Norway Maple, but do not have milky sap, and the twigs are more slender. The 3- to 6-inch blades on slender petioles are dark green and shiny above, lighter green beneath, with three to five blunt-pointed lobes having shallow, rounded sinuses between. The small samaras spread at about right angles from the slender stalk.

Sycamore Maple *(Acer pseudoplatanus)*

This tree from Europe is another large-leafed maple, which in size and habit of growth resembles the Norway Maple, and there are a number of horticultural forms. It grows to a height of 75 feet or more under favorable conditions, with a dense broadly spreading crown which casts heavy shade. In a dry climate it needs summer irrigation.

Figure 33 Sugar Maple

Leaves and fruit: The leaf blades are 4 to 7 inches long by about the same width, three- to five-lobed, with doubly serrate margins and sharply notched sinuses. The petioles are long and slender and the sap is not milky. Leaves are slightly heart-shaped at the base, glossy above and finely pubescent beneath. Yellow-green flowers are borne in drooping clusters 3 to 6 inches long after the leaves unfold. The fruit is glabrous, the samaras up to 2 inches long, the two spreading at 90° or less from a slender stalk.

[139]

Other maples which are occasionally seen include *A. buergerianum*, the Trident Maple, from Asia, a small tree, the leaves rounded at the base with entire margins and three-lobed near the apex; *A. campestre*, the Field Maple, from Europe, a small and rather dainty tree with small, somewhat leathery leaves, broadly five-lobed; *A. japonicum*, the Japanese Maple, a tree of moderate size, from Asia; and *A. negundo* cult. var. "Variegatum," the Silver Variegated Box Elder, a special clone of this compound-leaved tree with variegated silvery foliage. Those with green foliage are usually of the native Box Elder.

CASHEW FAMILY (Anacardiaceae)
(See also p. 71)

Only two members of this large family of mostly tropical trees are commonly seen in this region, although occasional shrubby specimens of *Rhus*, Sumac, may be present in special collections. One of the deciduous genera is *Cotinus*, with simple leaves; the other is *Pistacia*, which has graceful compound leaves.

Smoke Tree *(Cotinus coggygria)*

This tree from southern Europe is a small garden specimen 12 to 15 feet tall, with green or purplish foliage and smoky masses of fruit clusters which give it an interesting and unusual appearance. It is hardy, requires little care, and has few enemies. The larger *C. americanus*, from the eastern United States, is rarely seen here.

Leaves and fruit: The thin oval leaves, 2 to 3 inches long by about half as wide, are simple and entire, alternate in arrangement on slender petioles, and with entire margins. The form with light green leaves has striking foliage colors in autumn; that with purple foliage is of interest from spring to fall. Small yellowish flowers appear in large terminal clusters in early summer and develop into the feathery panicles which cover the crown in fall and give the tree its common name.

Chinese Pistache *(Pistacia chinensis)*

This is a good-sized timber tree in China, where it is native, and reaches a height of 60 feet or more. Although slow-growing, it is a hardy ornamental tree here, and thrives with minimum care in valley areas. It has notable beauty in street and highway plantings.

Leaves and fruit: The alternate, feather-compound leaves, 5 to 6 inches long, consist of five or six pairs of sessile leaflets each with rounded base, entire margins, and tapering to a slender point. The foliage is attractive from spring to fall: pink as the leaves unfold in spring, bright shiny green in summer, and brilliant red to orange in fall. Male and female flowers occur in inconspicuous clusters on separate trees, and foliage is denser on male trees. The fruits are dense clusters of small red or purple berries ¼ inch in diameter. The flesh of the nut is green, as in the edible pistachio nut, *P. vera*, from the Mediterranean, which is rarely cultivated here.

HORSECHESTNUT FAMILY (Hippocastanaceae)

This small family is characterized by opposite, palmate-compound leaves, showy flowers in erect spikes, and large shiny brown fruits enclosed in a thin green husk. It includes the native California Buckeye of the foothills, and Sweet Buckeye is a timber tree in the southeastern United States. About twenty species are widely distributed in the northern hemisphere.

Common Horsechestnut *(Aesculus hippocastanum)*

This is an attractive round-headed tree from the Balkan Peninsula which grows up to 60 feet tall. It has long been cultivated as a street and ornamental

[141]

tree. There are a number of horticultural varieties.

Leaves and fruit: The compound deep green leaves with long petioles are opposite in arrangement on the stout smooth twigs, which terminate in large sticky resinous buds. The leaves consist of seven obovate, sessile leaflets, 6 to 8 inches long by about 2 to 2½ inches wide, with toothed margins; they drop from the trees in early fall. Long spikes of densely packed white flowers are a showy feature in late spring, and ripen as spiny globular green pods containing a shiny brown nut resembling the eye of a buck.

Red Horsechestnut *(Aesculus x carnea)*

This is a smaller and slower-growing but very similar tree, up to 30 feet tall, a hybrid between *A. hippocastanum* and *A. pavia* of the south Atlantic Coast. It is now more frequently planted than is the Common Horsechestnut for the fine spikes of red flowers, 5 to 8 inches long, which bloom profusely in late spring. The cultivated variety "Briotii" has scarlet flowers.

Soapberry Family (Sapindaceae)

This large family, found mostly in tropical regions of both hemispheres, is both deciduous and evergreen. It usually has compound leaves, small flowers with ten stamens, and three-celled fruits with small seeds. *Alectryon excelsum,* Titoki, from New Zealand, is an evergreen species with ashlike compound leaves which is occasionally seen in areas near the coast. *Dodonaea viscosa* is a large bush with narrow purplish leaves up to 4 inches long, now quite popular in gardens.

Goldenrain Tree *(Koelreuteria paniculata)*

This is a hardy ornamental tree from China and Japan which grows up to 30 feet tall, with a rounded crown about half as broad. It thrives under a variety of soils from coastal to foothill areas, has few enemies, and requires a minimum of care.

Leaves and fruit: The compound alternate leaves are reddish in spring but become blue-green by summer. They are 10 to 14 inches long and consist of seven to fifteen lobed leaflets, 1½ to 3 inches long and half as wide, with toothed margins. The panicles of bright yellow flowers, ½ inch in diameter, are an attractive feature in early summer. They ripen as pendent, branched clusters 12 or more inches long, with papery, lantern-like capsules 1 to 2 inches long surrounding three black seeds. The fruits remain on the tree after the leaves are shed in early fall, and are so numerous they often seem to cover the entire crown. *K. formosana* is a larger tree with similar leaves and flowers, but the papery capsules are red, and it is less frost-hardy.

BASSWOOD OR LINDEN FAMILY (Tiliaceae)

This family includes some thirty genera of trees and shrubs with simple leaves in alternate arrangement, usually five-parted flowers, and small nutlike or drupe fruits. The genus *Tilia* includes a number of large handsome trees which are valuable for timber, nectar, and as ornamentals. About fourteen species are distributed throughout the northern hemisphere and there are also a number of hybrids.

Basswood or **American Linden** *(Tilia americana)*

This is a large and important timber tree of eastern North America which produces fine-grained, easily worked white lumber. In its optimum region it may reach 120 feet in height and 3 or more feet in diameter, but in this area it is usually not more than 50 feet tall, with large leaves, smooth branches and twigs, and light gray ridged trunk bark. The thumb-like red winter buds are sweet and mucilaginous to taste. It is a fine street and shade tree, but needs good soil and adequate summer moisture for best development.

Leaves and fruit: The simple dark green leaves are 4 to 6 inches long and nearly as wide, with long slender petioles. They are thin, asymmetrically heart-shaped at the base, tapering to a blunt point, and have toothed margins. They are in alternate arrangement on stout, smooth-barked twigs. In areas exposed to continuous winds off the ocean they become shredded. Small, fragrant, creamy-white flowers are borne in clusters on a slender stem which depends from a narrow 4- to 5-inch leafy bract. The flowers, eagerly sought by bees, yield a light honey of excellent flavor. They ripen as small nutlike globular berries which hang on the tree after the leaves turn yellow and fall.

Other lindens in cultivation here have similar foliage but vary in size, rate of growth, and leaves. All are fine ornamentals: *T. cordata*, the Littleleaf Linden, from Europe, with leaves up to 2½ inches long, heart-shaped and glaucous beneath; *T. japonica*, the Japanese Linden, with blue-green leaves up to 3 inches long; *T. tomentosa*, the Silver Linden, from Asia Minor, with short-petioled leaves, silvery-white pubescent beneath; and *T.* x *europea*, a hybrid from Europe, with 4-inch leaves, dull green above, shiny green beneath, with tufts of hairs in the axils of the veins, a fine street tree.

LOOSESTRIFE FAMILY (Lythraceae)

Many of the twenty-one genera in this family are found in the American tropics. A few are large trees. They have alternate or whorled leaves, and mostly tubular flowers with four to six petals; many have lavender or purple flowers. Only one species is in cultivation in this area.

[144]

Crape Myrtle (*Lagerstroemia indica*)

A decorative tree from China, this may grow up to 20 feet tall, and has been widely naturalized in mild climates around the world. Although often multiple-stemmed, it may be pruned to an attractive small tree distinguished by its smooth cream-colored bark and fine display of flowers in summer. It grows best in interior valleys with hot summers, and is less thrifty near the coast, where it is subject to mildew.

Leaves and fruit: The simple, opposite leaves without petioles are 1 to 2 inches long and half as wide, with entire margins, and often turn up in trough shape from the midrib. They are dark glossy green, with fine hairs on the veins beneath, and turn red or orange-yellow in fall. The flowers, with crinkly petals, are 1½ inches across, borne in showy terminal spikes, 6 to 8 inches long, in great profusion during late summer. The flowers range in color from white to rose or lavender, ripening as persistent small woody capsules on slender stalks.

EBONY FAMILY (Ebenaceae)

The six genera of trees and shrubs which belong in this family are found in temperate and warm parts of both hemispheres. The hard and valuable ebony lumber is from tropical members of the genus *Diospyros*.

Japanese Persimmon (*Diospyros kaki*)

This tree from China and Korea has been extensively planted in California for its ornamental foliage and fruits. It is a tree of moderate size, 25 to 40 feet tall, with a straight trunk and rounded crown of glossy foliage. Several varieties are grown in orchard form for the highly esteemed succulent fruits. It is hardy and indifferent to soil but does best on good sandy loam with some summer irrigation.

[145]

Leaves and fruit: The ovate, glossy dark green leaves are short-petioled, 3 to 7 inches long and half as wide, broadly rounded at the base. They are alternate in arrangement on the stout twigs, and slightly pubescent beneath. In fall they turn bright orange to red before dropping to display the persistent fruits which remain as decorative features during the fall. These are plump, ovoid or globular, 2 to 3 inches long, with smooth orange-yellow skin and decorative leafy sepals at the base. They may contain several flat seeds, but some varieties are now seedless, and when fully ripe are sweet and delicious.

American Persimmon *(Diospyros virginiana)*
This is a tree of the southeastern United States hardwood region, up to 50 feet tall, with smaller leaves and small astringent fruits containing many seeds. The foliage turns to attractive hues of orange and red in autumn. The dark brown trunk bark is intricately ridged. The tree is only occasionally seen in cultivation here, but is hardy and adaptable.

OLIVE FAMILY (Oleaceae)
(See also p. 80)
This family of opposite-leaved trees and shrubs includes such fine ornamentals as privet, jasmine, golden bell, fragrant olive, and lilac. Deciduous trees include the ashes, of which there are many important timber and ornamental species.

Arizona Ash *(Fraxinus velutina)*
This tree from the southwestern United States, and its smooth-leaved varieties, are now extensively planted in subdivision areas throughout this entire region. The species grows to a height of 30 to 40 feet, with a spreading crown. The tree is hardy, drought-resis-

tant, and indifferent to soils, and is better adapted to areas back from the coast.

Leaves and fruit: The opposite, compound leaves, 4 to 8 inches long, usually consist of five dull gray-green leaflets, about 1½ inches long by 1 inch wide, which taper both to tip and to the base and are sparingly toothed above the middle. They are usually quite pubescent, at least on the underside, and form a rather open crown, which turns yellow in fall. Male and female flowers appear on separate trees before the leaves. The tan-colored fruits, shaped like little canoe paddles, are an inch long, borne in drooping clusters on slender stalks.

The species is now less frequently planted than the two glossy-leaved varieties: *F. velutina* var *coriacea*, Montebello Ash, with shiny foliage, now commonly seen throughout southern California; and *F. velutina* "Modesto," the Modesto Ash, with glossy bright green foliage; the most popular clone, known as Stribling, is widely planted in this region. Since these are propagated vegetatively from male trees, they do not bear fruit.

Other ash species occasionally seen in cultivation include *F. americana*, the White Ash, from the middle western United States, the fine tall tree which produces excellent hardwood lumber, and which has stalked light green leaflets and brown buds on stout, smooth-barked twigs; *F. pennsylvanica*, the Green Ash, a smaller but hardier tree from the middle west with narrow lanceolate leaflets pubescent on the midrib beneath, commonly planted throughout the Great Basin country; *F. excelsior*, the European Ash, from southern Europe and Asia Minor, a fine tree up to 140 feet tall, with very long leaves and black buds; *F. ornus*, the Flowering Ash, a smaller tree from Europe, with daintier foliage and clusters of white

flowers borne with the leaves in early summer; and
F. holotricha, the Kimberly Blue Ash, a relatively new,
nicely formed, hardy variety of ash which is being
tested as a street tree throughout California, and is
apparently doing well with moderate care.

BIGNONIA FAMILY (Bignoniaceae)

This family of about a hundred genera includes
mostly opposite-leaved woody plants, chiefly of the
American tropics. They have showy trumpet-like flowers and flat, thin, symmetrically winged seeds borne
in a woody capsule. Trees of three genera are grown
in this region. One small tree of the southwestern deserts, *Chilopsis linearis,* the Desert Willow, with blue
or lilac flowers striped with yellow inside, and long
slender leaves, grows near springs and in river bot-
toms. It is occasionally planted in warm, dry areas.

Western Catalpa *(Catalpa speciosa)*

This tree from the middle western United States
is a hardy species, up to 75 feet tall. The good-sized
trunk is clothed in fibrous light brown bark. Its light,
strong, and easily worked wood is durable in the soil,
and so has been used for fenceposts. It is popular as
a street and highway tree and park specimen because
of its striking display of flowers in early summer.

Leaves and fruit: The large light green leaves,
opposite in arrangement on the stout twigs, are up to
12 inches long, heart-shaped at the base with entire
margins, and taper to a long pointed tip. They are
shiny above and finely hairy beneath, with petioles
4 to 6 inches long. The flowers, 2½ inches across, are
white to cream-colored with brown spots on the petals,
and appear in open panicles up to 6 inches long. The
pendent fruits, sometimes called "Indian cigars," are
10 to 18 inches long by ½ inch in diameter. When
ripe they split open to release many double-winged

[148]

seeds about an inch long, with rounded wings fringed on the ends.

Figure 34 Western Catalpa

Common Catalpa *(Catalpa bignonioides)*

This is a smaller, less hardy species up to 50 feet tall. It is similar to the preceding species, but has smaller leaves which taper to a blunt point, flowers with yellow and purple spots, and slender capsules 6 to 12 inches long. Both species are commonly planted as street trees and in parks.

Green Ebony or **Sharpleaf Jacaranda** *(Jacaranda acutifolia)*

This tree from Brazil is a spectacularly beautiful street and ornamental tree which grows to a height of about 50 feet and has a spreading, rounded crown of foliage. It makes a fine display of flowers in late spring, but is not fully frost-hardy in this region. However, some good specimens may be seen in sheltered situations not far from the coast.

Leaves and fruit: The feathery light green leaves are opposite and twice-compound, up to 20 inches long, composed of twenty to forty pinnae in opposite arrangement on the central rachis. Each has a large number of tiny, sharp-pointed leaflets about ⅓ inch long except the terminal one, which is ½ inch or more in length. The tubular bluish-lavender flowers are 2 inches long, densely clustered in terminal panicles up to 8 inches long. They ripen as thick, woody, purse-shaped flat pods which turn shiny brown when ripe and contain hard seeds. They persist on the tree for some months. In this area the trees drop their leaves at irregular times depending on the weather; so they may be leafless in late summer.

FIGWORT FAMILY (Scrophulariaceae)

This large family includes some 180 genera of herbs, shrubs, and trees found in temperate and tropical regions of both hemispheres. Many small plants are used as ornamentals, and some for medicinal purposes. Only one deciduous tree is in cultivation here.

Empress Tree *(Paulownia tomentosa)*

This tree from China has much the same appearance and habit of growth as catalpa, reaching a height of about 40 feet, with large leaves and panicles of showy flowers. It has escaped from cultivation at several points in the eastern United States south of New York, and usually sprouts vigorously from the roots if the top is killed back by frost. It is frost-hardy in this region, but is apt to suffer damage from sunburn on the southwest side in valley areas. This should be taken into account in pruning practice. The tree succeeds best on sandy loam with summer irrigation and in a partially shaded situation. It has relative immunity from diseases and pests.

Leaves and fruit: The large broad-bladed leaves are opposite in arrangement, with entire or very shallowly lobed margins, 12 inches long by 8 inches wide, densely pubescent both on blades and on the long petioles. The base of the blade is more heart-shaped than in the catalpa. The fragrant violet flowers, up to 2 inches across, striped with yellow inside, occur in showy terminal clusters 8 to 10 inches long in spring before the leaves unfold. These ripen as oval, woody, capsular fruits up to 1½ inches long and half as wide, containing many tiny winged seeds. The plump pods persist in clusters on the tree after the leaves fall.

CHECK LIST OF INTRODUCED TREES

CONIFEROUS TREES
PINE FAMILY (PINACEAE)
Santa Lucia Fir (*Abies bracteata*)
White Fir (*Abies concolor*)
Nordmann Fir (*Abies nordmanniana*)
Spanish Fir (*Abies pinsapo*)
Atlas Cedar (*Cedrus atlantica*)
Deodar Cedar (*Cedrus deodara*)
Lebanon Cedar (*Cedrus libanensis*)
Beach or Shore Pine (*Pinus contorta*)
Dwarf Pine (*Pinus mugo*)
Scot's Pine (*Pinus sylvestris*)
Japanese Black Pine (*Pinus thunbergii*)
Japanese Red Pine (*Pinus densiflora*)
Austrian Pine (*Pinus nigra*)
Italian Stone Pine (*Pinus pinea*)
Cluster or Maritime Pine (*Pinus pinaster*)
Aleppo Pine (*Pinus halepensis*)
Canary Island Pine (*Pinus canariensis*)
Weeping Mexican Pine (*Pinus patula*)
Torrey Pine (*Pinus torreyana*)
Bhutan or Himalayan Pine (*Pinus wallichiana*)
Colorado Blue Spruce (*Picea pungens*)
Norway Spruce (*Picea abies*)
Himalayan or Weeping Spruce (*Picea smithiana*)
Sitka or Tideland Spruce (*Picea sitchensis*)
Oriental Spruce (*Picea orientalis*)

REDWOOD FAMILY (TAXODIACEAE)
Sugi or Cryptomeria (*Cryptomeria japonica*)
China Fir (*Cunninghamia lanceolata*)
Umbrella Pine (*Sciadopitys verticillata*)
Sierra Redwood (*Sequoia gigantea*)
Bald Cypress (*Taxodium distichum*)
Dawn Redwood (*Metasequoia glyptostroboides*)

CYPRESS and JUNIPER FAMILY (CUPRESSACEAE)
Port Orford Cedar or Lawson Cypress (*Chamaecyparis lawsoniana*)
Hinoki Cypress (*Chamaecyparis obtusa*)
Sawara Cypress (*Chamaecyparis pisifera*)
Arizona Cypress (*Cupressus glabra*)
Italian Cypress (*Cupressus sempervirens*)
Giant Arborvitae (*Thuja plicata*)
American Arborvitae (*Thuja occidentalis*)
Chinese Arborvitae (*Thuja orientalis*)
False Arborvitae (*Thujopsis dolobrata*)
Chinese Juniper (*Juniperus chinensis*)
Eastern Red Cedar (*Juniperus virginiana*)
Canary Island Juniper (*Juniperus cedrus*)
Savin (*Juniperus sabina*)

GINKGO FAMILY (GINKGOACEAE)
Maidenhair Tree (*Ginkgo biloba*)

ARAUCARIA FAMILY (ARAUCARIACEAE)
Monkey Puzzle (*Araucaria araucana*)
Bunya Bunya (*Araucaria bidwilli*)
Norfolk Island Pine (*Araucaria heterophylla*)

YEW FAMILY (TAXACEAE)
English Yew (*Taxus baccata*)
Japanese Yew (*Taxus cuspidata*)

PODOCARPUS FAMILY (PODOCARPACEAE)
Yew Podocarpus (*Podocarpus macrophylla*)
Fern Podocarpus (*Podocarpus gracilior*)

MONOCOTYLEDONS: PALMS AND THEIR ALLIES
PALM FAMILY (PALMACEAE)
Canary Island Palm (*Phoenix canariensis*)
Senegal Date Palm (*Phoenix reclinata*)
Wine or Syrup Palm (*Jubaea chilensis*)
Windmill Palm (*Trachycarpus fortunei*)
California Fan Palm (*Washingtonia filifera*)
Mexican Fan Palm (*Washingtonia robusta*)
Chinese Fan Palm (*Livistona chinensis*)

LILY FAMILY (LILIACEAE)
Green Dracena (*Cordyline australis*)

[153]

Blue Dracena (*Cordyline indivisa*)
Dragon Tree (*Dracaena draco*)
Abyssinian Banana (*Musa ensete*)

DICOTYLEDONS: BROAD-LEAVED TREES;HARDWOODS
EVERGREEN BROADLEAF TREES
MYRTLE FAMILY (MYRTACEAE)
Blue Gum (*Eucalyptus globulus*)
Red Gum (*Eucalyptus globulus*)
Forest Red Gum (*Eucalyptus tereticornis*)
Moitch or Desert Gum (*Eucalyptus rudis*)
Manna Gum (*Eucalyptus viminalis*)
Scarlet Gum (*Eucalyptus ficifolia*)
Red Ironbark or Mugga (*Eucalyptus sideroxylon*)
Narrow-leaved Ironbark (*Eucalyptus crebra*)
Red Box (*Eucalyptus polyanthemos*)
Yellow Box (*Eucalytus melliodora*)
Silver-leaved Gum (*Eucalyptus pulverulenta*)
Swamp Messmate (*Eucalyptus robusta*)
Australian Bush Cherry (*Syzygium paniculatum* or *Eugenia myrtifolia*)
Cajeput Tree (*Melaleuca leucadendra*)
Brilliant Bottle-brush (*Callistemon citrinus* or *C. lanceolatus*)
Australian Tea Tree (*Leptospermum laevigatum*)
Manuka Tea Tree (*Leptospermum scoparium*)
Brush Box (*Tristania conferta*)
Brown Apple (*Angophora costata*)

BEAN or PEA FAMILY (LEGUMINOSAE)
Green Wattle (*Acacia decurrens*)
Silver Wattle (*Acacia decurrens dealbata*)
Black Wattle (*Acacia decurrens mollis*)
Cootamundra Wattle (*Acacia baileyana*)
Blackwood Acacia (*Acacia melanoxylon*)
Carob or St. John's Bread (*Ceratonia siliqua*)

LAUREL FAMILY (LAURACEAE)
Grecian Laurel or Bay (*Laurus nobilis*)
Camphor Tree (*Cinnamomum camphora*)
Avocado (*Persea americana*)
Bellota Tree (*Cryptocarya miersii*)

CASHEW FAMILY (ANACARDIACEAE)
California Pepper (*Schinus molle*)

[154]

Brazilian Pepper (*Schinus terebinthefolius*)
Cabrera or Tree Pepper (*Schinus polygamus*)

PITTOSPORUM FAMILY (PITTOSPORACEAE)
Orange Pittosporum (*Pittosporum undulatum*)

PROTEA FAMILY (PROTEACEAE)
Silk Oak (*Grevillea robusta*)

MAGNOLIA FAMILY (MAGNOLIACEAE)
Southern Magnolia (*Magnolia grandiflora*)

STAFF-TREE FAMILY (CELASTRACEAE)
Mayten Tree (*Maytenus boaria*)

MULBERRY FAMILY (MORACEAE)
Moreton Bay Fig (*Ficus macrophylla*)
Indian Laurel Fig (*Ficus retusa*)

HOLLY FAMILY (AQUIFOLIACEAE)
English Holly (*Ilex aquifolium*)
Chinese Holly (*Ilex cornuta*)

HEATH FAMILY (ERICACEAE)
Strawberry Tree (*Arbutus unedo*)

OLIVE FAMILY (OLEACEAE)
Common or Mission Olive (*Olea europaea*)
Glossy Privet (*Ligustrum lucidum*)
Common Privet (*Ligustrum vulgare*)
California Privet (*Ligustrum ovalifolium*)
Shamel or Evergreen Ash (*Fraxinus uhdei*)

ROSE FAMILY (ROSACEAE)
Loquat (*Eriobotrya japonica*)
Chinese Photinia (*Photinia serrulata*)
Carolina Cherry (*Prunus caroliniana*)
English or Cherry Laurel (*Prunus laurocerasus*)
Portugal Laurel (*Prunus lusitanica*)
Catalina Cherry (*Prunus lyonii*)
Catalina or Island Ironwood (*Lyonothamnus floribundus* var. *asplenifolius*)

Soapbark Tree (*Quillaja saponaria*)
Evergreen Pear (*Pyrus kawakamii*)

BEECH-OAK FAMILY (FAGACEAE)
Cork Oak (*Quercus suber*)
Holm or Holly Oak (*Quercus ilex*)

BEEFWOOD FAMILY (CASUARINACEAE)
Beefwood or River She Oak (*Casuarina cunninghamiana*)
She Oak or Beefwood (*Casuarina stricta*)

STERCULEA FAMILY (STERCULACEAE)
Kurrajong Bottle Tree (*Brachychiton populneum*)

TAMARISK FAMILY (TAMARICACEAE)
Athel or Desert Tamarisk (*Tamarix aphylla*)

RUE FAMILY (RUTACEAE)
White Sapote (*Casimiroa edulis*)
Sweet Orange (*Citrus sinensis*)
Wilga (*Geijera parviflora*)

DECIDUOUS BROADLEAF TREES
WALNUT FAMILY (JUGLANDACEAE)
English Walnut (*Juglans regia*)
American Black Walnut (*Juglans nigra*)
Butternut (*Juglans cinerea*)
Pecan (*Carya illinoensis*)
Chinese Wingnut (*Pterocarya stenoptera*)

PLANE TREE or SYCAMORE FAMILY (PLATANACEAE)
London Plane (*Platanus* x *acerifolia*)

WILLOW FAMILY (SALICACEAE)
Weeping Willow (*Salix babylonica*)
Curl-leaf Willow (*Salix babylonica* "Crispa")
White Poplar or Abele (*Populus alba*)
Common Cottonwood (*Populus deltoides*)
Lombardy Poplar (*Populus nigra* "Italica")

BIRCH FAMILY (BETULACEAE)
European White Birch (*Betula verrucosa*)
Giant Filbert (*Corylus maxima*)

BEECH-OAK FAMILY (FAGACEAE)
Spanish Chestnut (*Castanea sativa*)
American Chestnut (*Castanea dentata*)
Chinese Chestnut (*Castanea mollissima*)
European Beech (*Fagus sylvatica*)
English Oak (*Quercus robur*)
Turkey Oak (*Quercus cerris*)
Bur Oak (*Quercus macrocarpa*)
White Oak (*Quercus alba*)
Northern Red Oak (*Quercus rubra*)
Scarlet Oak (*Quercus coccinea*)
Pin Oak (*Quercus palustris*)

ELM FAMILY (ULMACEAE)
American Elm (*Ulmus americana*)
English Elm (*Ulmus procera*)
Scotch or Wych Elm (*Ulmus glabra*)
Chinese Elm (*Ulmus parvifolia*)
Siberian Elm (*Ulmus pumila*)

HACKBERRY FAMILY (CELTIS)
European Hackberry (*Celtis australis*)
Chinese Hackberry (*Celtis sinensis*)
American Hackberry (*Celtis occidentalis*)
Sugarberry (*Celtis laevigata*)
Sawleaf Zelkova (*Zelkova serrata*)

MULBERRY FAMILY (MORACEAE)
White Mulberry (*Morus alba*)
Russian Mulberry (*Morus alba* "Tatarica")
Black Mulberry (*Morus nigra*)
Red Mulberry (*Morus rubra*)
Paper Mulberry (*Broussonetia papyrifera*)
Common Fig (*Ficus carica*)
Osage Orange (*Maclura pomifera*)

MAGNOLIA FAMILY (MAGNOLIACEAE)
Tulip Tree or Yellow Poplar (*Liriodendron tulipifera*)

WITCH HAZEL FAMILY (HAMAMELIDACEAE)
Sweet Gum (*Liquidambar styraciflua*)

ROSE FAMILY (ROSACEAE)
Cherries (*Prunus* sp.)

[157]

English Hawthorne (*Crataegus oxycantha*)
Washington Thorn (*Crataegus phaenopyrum*)
Lavalle or Carriere Thorn (*Crataegus* x *lavallei*)
Crabapples (*Malus* sp.)
European Mountain Ash (*Sorbus aucuparia*)

BEAN or PEA FAMILY (LEGUMINOSAE)
Black Locust (*Robinia pseudoacacia*)
Hairy Locust (*Robinia neomexicana*)
Honey Locust (*Gleditsia triacanthos*)
Moraine Locust (*Gleditsia triacanthos* "Inermis")
Mimosa or Silk Tree (*Albizia julibrissin*)
Golden Chain or Bead Tree (*Laburnum anagyroides*)
Japanese Pagoda Tree (*Sophora japonica*)
Redbuds (*Cercis* sp.)
Yellow Wood (*Cladrastis lutea*)
Orchid Tree (*Bauhinia purpurea*)
Jerusalem Thorn (*Parkinsonia aculeata*)

QUASSIA FAMILY (SIMARUBACEAE)
Tree of Heaven (*Ailanthus altissima*)

MAHOGANY FAMILY (MELIACEAE)
Texas Umbrella (*Melia azedarach* "Umbraculifera")

MAPLE FAMILY (ACERACEAE)
Silver Maple (*Acer saccharinum*)
Red or Swamp Maple (*Acer rubrum*)
Japanese Maple (*Acer palmatum*)
Norway Maple (*Acer platanoides*)
Sugar Maple (*Acer saccharum*)
Sycamore Maple (*Acer pseudoplatanus*)

CASHEW FAMILY (ANACARDIACEAE)
Smoke Tree (*Cotinus coggygria*)
Chinese Pistache (*Pistacia chinensis*)

HORSECHESTNUT FAMILY (HIPPOCASTANACEAE)
Common Horsechestnut (*Aesculus hippocastanum*)
Red Horsechestnut (*Aesculus* x *carnea*)

SOAPBERRY FAMILY (SAPINDACEAE)
Goldenrain Tree (*Koelreuteria paniculata*)

BASSWOOD or LINDEN FAMILY (TILIACEAE)
Basswood or American Linden (*Tilia americana*)

LOOSESTRIFE FAMILY (LYTHRACEAE)
Crape Myrtle (*Lagerstroemia indica*)

EBONY FAMILY (EBENACEAE)
Japanese Persimmon (*Diospyros kaki*)
American Persimmon (*Diospyros virginiana*)

OLIVE FAMILY (OLEACEAE)
Arizona Ash (*Fraxinus velutina*)

BIGNONIA FAMILY (BIGNONIACEAE)
Western Catalpa (*Catalpa speciosa*)
Common Catalpa (*Catalpa bignonioides*)
Sharpleaf Jacaranda (*Jacaranda acutifolia*)

FIGWORT FAMILY (SCROPHULARIACEAE)
Empress Tree (*Paulownia tomentosa*)